W. D. GANN

45 Years In Wall Street

ISBN: 978-1-63923-513-1

Printed: October 2022

Cover Art By: Amit Paul

Published and Distributed By:
Lushena Books
607 Country Club Drive, Unit E
Bensenville, IL 60106
www.lushenabks.com

ISBN: 978-1-63923-513-1

W. D. Gann

45 YEARS
IN WALL STREET

A Review of the 1937 Panic and 1942 Panic,
1946 Bull Market with New Time Rules
and Percentage Rules with Charts
for Determining the Trend
on Stocks

By

WILLIAM D. GANN

DEDICATED

To

The Memory of

SADIE H. GANN

A Good Wife and a Wonderful Mother

FOREWORD

In 1910 at the request of friends I wrote a small booklet entitled "Speculation a Profitable Profession." In this booklet I gave the rules that helped me to make a success in my personal trading.

January, 1923, I wrote, "Truth of the Stock Tape" to help those who were trying to help themselves in speculation and investment trading. This book was favorably received by the public and many proclaimed it my Masterpiece. The book fulfilled its mission as evidenced by letters from grateful readers. After predicting the great panic in 1929 there was a call for a new book to bring "Truth of the Stock Tape" up to date. I answered that call in the early part of 1930 by writing "Wall Street Stock Selector" giving my readers the benefit of practical experience in which I developed new rules since 1923. In "Wall Street Stock Selector" I predicted the "Investors Panic," and said that it would be the greatest panic the world had ever known. This prediction was fulfilled by the panic which ended in July, 1932, with some stocks declining to the lowest levels they had reached for the past 40 to 50 years.

A great advance followed the 1932 panic and my rules helped many people to make substantial profits.

In 1935 satisfied readers asked me to write a new book. I responded to that call by writing my third book "New Stock Trend Detector" in the latter part of 1935, giving the benefit of my experience and new and practical rules which I had discovered.

Since 1935 many changes have taken place; the market passed through the panic of 1937 which was forecast by me. The decline ended in March, 1928, and a minor Bull Market followed to November 10, 1938.

The second World War started September 1,˙1939, and the United States entered the war in December, 1941. After we were in the war a further liquidation in stocks occurred and final lows were reached April 28, 1942, when stocks sold below the low level of 1938 at the lowest levels since 1932.

From the lows in 1942 a prolonged advance followed

which continued after the end of the Japanese War in August, 1945.

1946, May 29, stocks sold at the highest level they had reached since 1929. My rules and my forecast called the top of this advance and the sharp decline which followed to October 30, 1946, when final low was reached.

Fourteen years have passed since writing my last book and I have gained more knowledge through actual market operations. The world is upset and confused; investors and traders are puzzled over the business depression and the decline in the stock market. Many have written requesting me to write a new book. With the desire to help others I have written "45 Years in Wall Street" giving the benefit of my experience and my new discoveries to aid others in these difficult times. I am now in my 72nd year; fame would do me no good. I have more income than I can spend for my needs, therefore, my only object in writing this new book is to give to others the most valuable gift possible—KNOWLEDGE! If a few find the way to make safer investments my object will have been accomplished and satisfied readers will be my reward.

W. D. GANN.

July 2, 1949

INTRODUCTION

In 1926 I read "Truth of the Stock Tape," written by W. D. Gann in 1923. To me it was a masterpiece. Then in 1927 I met Mr. Gann and since then I have read all the books he has written. The rules he has laid down have greatly benefited me when times were good, also when they were trying.

In one place he says "Remember when you make a trade, you can be wrong, therefore place a stop loss order for your protection." Another rule says, "When in doubt, get out of the market." Then again he says, "When you have nothing but hope to hold on to, get out of the market." That I am writing this, should indicate I have followed these rules and others in his books, and they have paid off.

It has been my pleasure and privilege to read Mr. Gann's latest book, "Forty-Five Years in Wall Street," before it goes to press, and I commend it to others. What he has written here is the result of many years of research and study. He is the only man I ever knew who I thought had worked as much as Mr. Thomas Edison.

In this his latest book, the rule on short time period price correction is a valuable one to any investor. Time period rules, three day and nine point charts and anniversary dates, are new discoveries by Mr. Gann, that I have never read about from anyone else.

This book contains rules that will help one make profits and keep them, if the rules are learned and applied without hope or fear.

CLARENCE KIRVEN.

July, 1949

45 YEARS IN WALL STREET
CONTENTS

CONTENTS (Continued)

CHARTS

45 YEARS
IN WALL STREET

CHAPTER I

IS IT MORE DIFFICULT TO MAKE PROFITS NOW THAN BEFORE 1932?

Many people write me and ask this question. My answer is—No, you can make just as great profits now as you ever could, provided you select the right stocks to buy and sell. Changed conditions have changed market actions somewhat. The laws passed by the government regulate trading in stocks and require higher margin. The income tax laws make it necessary to trade for the long pull swings in order to escape paying too much income tax. It no longer pays to try to scalp the market because swings in a short period of time do not warrant it. Remaining in the broker's office and trying to read the tape is out of date. You will benefit by spending your time making up charts and studying them.

Many stocks that have been listed for a long time have become seasoned and move more slowly. This cuts out the possibilities for quick profits in a short period of time. There is no longer a large list of stocks selling at high prices above $100 per share and making wide fluctuations.

1949, June 14, when stocks reached extreme Low there were about 1,100 issues traded in that day. There were only 112 stocks selling above $100 per share. Many of these were preferred stocks held by investors and this class of stocks moves in a narrow range. On June 14 there were 315 stocks selling below 20, 202 selling below 10, and 83 selling below $5.00 per share, making a total of 600 selling below 20 per share, or more than 50% of the total issues traded. With so many stocks selling at Low Levels, you can only make money by taking a long-pull trading position.

During recent years many of the high priced stocks have declared stock dividends, splitting up the stock and putting more stocks in the low price range.

Larger Profits on Same Amount of Capital

You can make more money today than you could several years ago using the same amount of capital. For example: When a stock was selling at $100 per share and you bought 100 shares you had to put up $10,000 or pay for it outright. And at the time you could buy it on the 50% margin, if it advanced 10 points, you made a profit of $1,000 or 20% on your capital. At the present time, suppose you should buy 1,000 shares of a stock selling at $10 per share on a 50% margin, this would require $5,000 capital. If the stock advances 5 points you will have made a profit of $5,000 or 100% on your capital investment. With so many stocks selling at Low Levels with good prospects for future enhancement, you have opportunities for making profits just as fast today as ever before.

Volume of Sales Smaller

The total volume of stocks traded on the New York Stock Exchange during recent years is much smaller. This is because people buy stocks and hold them longer. There are no longer any pools or manipulation in stocks since the passing of the Security Exchange Regulations. This does not mean that there cannot be Big Bull markets and large advances in the future. As time goes by stocks pass into the hands of investors who hold them for a long period of time. The floating supply is gradually absorbed. Then, when something suddenly happens to start a buying wave, buyers find the supply of stocks scarce and have to bid them up. It always happens that the higher prices go, the more people want to buy. This causes a final grand rush and a rapid advance in the last stages of a Bull Market. History repeats on Wall Street and what has happened in the past will happen again in the future.

In January, 1946, the U. S. Government made a rule compelling everyone who bought stocks to put up 100% margin, or in other words, pay for them outright. Stocks were already selling at very High Levels and had been advancing for three and a half years. Did this ruling by the government stop the public from buying stocks? It did not. The Averages advanced more than 20 points and the advance lasted five months longer to May 29, 1946, when final High was reached, which proves that the government could not stop the advance in stocks as long as the people were in the mood to buy. In fact, a lot of traders believe that the government took this action because it thought there would be a runaway advance in stocks and traders believing this continued to buy stocks regardless of the margin required. My experience has taught me that nothing can stop the Trend as long as the Time Cycle shows Up-Trend. Nothing can stop its decline as long as the Time Cycle shows Down. Stocks can and do go Up on bad news and go Down on good news.

1949 in March, the government reduced the marginal requirements on stock to 50% margin. Many people thought this was very bullish and that it would start a Bull Market, but it did not. Stocks rallied for two days to March 30, then declined over 18 points on the Averages until June 14. They went down because the Trend was down. The Time Cycle had not run out for Bottom.

Cross Currents in Stocks

In recent years the market has been more mixed than for a long time. Some groups of stocks advance while others decline at the same time. This is due to various causes and conditions in the different industries. You can determine these cross currents and get the Trend of any individual stock if you keep up a Monthly High and Low Chart and study it and apply the rules which I give you.

Why You Have Lost Money in Stocks
AND
How to Make It Back

Why do the great majority of people who buy and sell stocks lose? There are three main reasons:

1. They overtrade or buy and sell too much for their capital.

2. They do not place stop loss orders or limit their losses.

3. Lack of Knowledge. This is the most important reason of all.

Most people buy a stock because they hope it will go up and they will make profits. They buy on tips, or what someone else thinks, without any concrete knowledge of their own that the stock will advance. Thus they entered the market wrong and did not recognize this mistake or attempt to correct it until too late. Finally they sell because they fear the stock will go lower and often they sell out near low levels, getting out at the wrong time, making two mistakes, getting in the market at the wrong time and getting out at the wrong time. One mistake could have been prevented, they could have gotten out right after getting in wrong. They do not realize that operating in Stocks and Commodities is a business or a profession, the same as engineering or the medical profession.

Why You Should Learn to Determine the Trend of the Market

You may have tried to follow market letters and like many others either lost money or failed to make profits, because the market letters gave a list of too many stocks to buy or sell and you picked the wrong one and lost. A smart man cannot follow another man blindly even though the other man is right, because you cannot have confidence and act on advice when you do not know what it is based on. You will be able to act with confidence and make profits when you can SEE and KNOW for YOURSELF why STOCKS should go UP or DOWN.

That is why you should study all of my rules and make up charts for yourself on the individual stocks, as well as the averages. If you do this you will prepare yourself to act independent of the advice of others, because you will know from Time-Tested Rules what the trend of the market should be.

CHAPTER II

RULES FOR TRADING IN STOCKS

To make a success in trading in stocks you must get the knowledge first; you must learn before you lose. Many traders go into the stock market without any knowledge and lose a large part of their capital before they learn that it is necessary to go through a period of preparation before they start trading. I am giving you the benefit of more than 45 years of experience in the stock market and laying down rules which, if you learn and follow, will make you a success.

The first thing for you to realize is that when you make a trade you can be *wrong;* then you *must know* what to do to *correct* your *mistake.* The way to do that is to *limit* your *risk* by *placing* a *Stop* Loss Order 1, 2 or 3 points below the price at which you buy. Then if you are wrong you will automatically be sold out and will be in position to enter the market again when you have a definite indication. *Do not guess;* make a trade on definite rules and according to definite indications based on the rules which I lay down; this will give you a better chance to make a success.

Read all of the rules and examples in my books, "Truth of the Stock Tape", "Wall Street Stock Selector" and "New Stock Trend Detector", and study 12 and 24 rules which are bound with this book "45 Years in Wall Street". The rules are good and will benefit you if you study them. Remember that you can never learn too much. Always be ready and willing to learn something new; never have a fixed idea that you know it all. If you do, you will not make any more progress. Times and conditions change and you must learn to change with them. Human nature does not change and that is the reason history repeats and stocks act very much the same under certain conditions year after year and in the various cycles of time.

Rule 1. Determining the Trend

Determine the trend of the Dow-Jones 30 Industrial Averages or the 15 public utilities averages or the average on any group of stocks that you intend to trade in, then select the stock in the group in which you want to trade and see if its Trend indications conform to the Trend indicated by the Averages. You should use the 3-Day Chart for the Averages and the 9-Point Average Swing Chart as outlined later in the book, and apply all of the rules for determining the right time to buy or sell.

Rule 2. Buy at Single, Double and Triple Bottoms

Buy at Double and Triple Bottoms or on Single Bottoms when they are nearer previous Old Bottoms or Tops or resistance levels. Remember the rule: Tops or ceilings which are selling points become floors, supports or buying points after these tops have been crossed and the market reacts to them, or sells slightly below them. Sell at or against Single, Double or Triple Tops and, remember, that after an Old Top is broken by several points and the market rallies up to or near it again, it becomes a selling point. After you have made a trade, determine the proper and safe place to place a Stop Loss Order, and give it to your broker immediately. If you do not know where to place a Stop Loss Order, do not make the trade.

Do not overlook the fact that the 4th time the averages or an individual stock reaches the same level it is not as safe to sell, because it nearly always goes through. Reverse this rule at the bottom. When stocks decline to the same level the 4th time in most cases it breaks the bottom and continues down.

The Meaning of Double Tops and Bottoms

A Double Top on the Averages can be in a range of 3 to 5 points. However, most Double Tops form in a range of from 1 to 2 points except at great extremes. The same way at an extreme bottom. If there has been a previous bottom around this same level many years back, the Averages can decline 4 to 5 points below the previous bottom without indicating that they are going lower, and this can become a Double or a Triple Bottom.

Individual stocks usually make a Double Top in a 2 to 3 point range and sometimes within a 1 to 2 point range. The same at the bottom; they make a Double Bottom in a 2 to 3 point range and sometimes the range is only 1 to 2 points below the different bottoms. Stop Loss Orders should be plaeed on individual stocks 1 to 3 points above Double and Triple Tops, depending upon how high stocks are selling. Stop Loss Orders should be placed under Double and Triple Bottoms 1 to 3 points away.

A Triple Top or Bottom occurs when the Averages or an individual stock has reached the same level the 3rd time. This is often the safest place to buy or sell because the market moves away from a Triple Top or a Triple Bottom much faster.

Rule 3. Buy and Sell on Percentages

Buy or sell on a 50% decline from any high level or a 50% advance from any low level so long as these reactions or rallies are with the main trend. You can use the percentage of the individual stocks as well as the percentage of the Averages to determine the resistance levels and buying and selling points. You can use 3 to 5 per cent, next 10 to 12 per cent, next 20 to 25 per cent, 33 to 37 per cent, 45 to 50 per cent, 62 to 67 per cent, 72 to 78 per cent and 85 to 87 per cent. The most important resistance levels are 50% and 100% and the proportionate parts of 100%. (See examples under Chapter on Percentages of High and Low Prices.)

Rule 4. Buy and Sell on 3 Weeks' Advance or Decline

Buy on a 3 weeks' reaction or decline in a Bull Market when the main trend is up, as this is the average reaction in a strong Bull Market. In a Bear Market sell on a rally of around 3 weeks after you know the trend is down.

After a market advances or declines 30 days or more, the next time period to watch for tops and bottoms is around

6 to 7 weeks which will be a buying or selling level, protected, of course, with Stop Loss Orders according to resistance levels. After a market rallies or declines more than 45 to 49 days, the next time period is around 60 to 65 days which is about the greatest average time that a Bear Market rallies or a Bull Market reacts.

Rule 5. Market Moves in Sections

Stock market campaigns move in 3 to 4 Sections or waves. Never consider that the market has reached final top when it makes the first section in a move up, because if it is a real Bull Market it will run at least 3 Sections and possibly 4 before a final high is reached.

In a Bear Market, or declining market, never consider the market as final bottom when it makes the first decline or Section because it will run 3 and possibly 4 Sections before the Bear campaign is over.

Rule 6. Buy or Sell on 5 to 7 Point Moves

Buy or sell individual stocks on reactions of 5 to 7 points. When a market is strong, reactions will run 5 to 7 points but— will not decline as much as 9 or 10 points. By studying the Industrial Averages you will see how often a rally or reaction runs less than 10 points. However, it is important to watch 10 to 12 point rallies or declines for buying or selling levels on the average. The next important point to watch is 18 to 21 points up or down from any important Top or Bottom. Reactions of this kind in the Averages often indicate the end of a move.

When to Take Profits—After you have bought stocks or sold them, the next thing you need to know is when to take profit. Follow the rules and do not take profits until there is a definite indication of a change in trend.

Rule 7. Volume of Sales

Study the total volume of sales on the New York Stock Exchange in connection with the time periods and study the rules under volume of sales later on in the book. Study the volume of sales on individual stocks based on the rules given, as the volume of sales will help in determining when the trend is changing.

Rule 8. Time Periods

The time factor and time periods are most important in determining a change in trend because Time can over balance Price and when the Time is up the Volume of sales will increase and force prices higher or lower.

Dates for Change in Trend—The stock market averages and individual stocks follow a seasonal change in trend which varies in different years, but by knowing the important dates and watching them you will be able to determine a change in trend very quickly by applying all the other rules. The important dates are as follows:

January 7 to 10, and 19 to 24. These are the most important at the beginning of the year, and changes in trend that last for several weeks, and sometimes several months, occur around these dates. Check the records and prove it for yourself.

February 3 to 10, and 20 to 25. These are next important to the dates in January.

March 20 to 27. Minor changes occur around this date and sometimes major tops or bottoms occur.

April 7 to 12, and 20 to 25. Not as important as January and February, but the latter part of April is often quite important for a change in trend.

May 3 to 10, and 21 to 28. The changes this month are of as great importance as those that occur in January and February, and many major Tops and Bottoms have occurred around these dates in the past and a change in trend has taken place.

June 10 to 15, and 21 to 27. Minor changes in trend occur around these dates and in some years extreme highs and extreme lows occur. Example: 1948, June 14, extreme high; 1949, June 14, extreme low, up to the time of this writing.

July 7 to 10, 21 to 27. This month is next in importance to January because it is at the middle of the year when dividend payments occur and seasonal changes and crop conditions have some effect on the change in trend of stocks.

August 5 to 8, and 14 to 20. This month is as important in some ways as February for change. Check the back records and you will see how important changes occur around these dates.

September 3 to 10, and 21 to 28. These periods are the most important of any in the year, especially for Tops, or final highs in a Bull Market, as more highs have occurred in September than any other month. Some minor changes, both up and down, have occurred around these dates.

October 7 to 14, and 21 to 30. These periods are quite important and some major changes have occurred between these dates. They should always be watched if a market has been declining or advancing for some time.

November 5 to 10, and 20 to 30. These are very important for changes in trend as a study in past history will prove. In election years a change in trend often occurs in the early part of the month, and in other years low prices are recorded between the 20th and 30th.

December 3 to 10, and 15 to 24. The latter period and running into the January period for a change in trend has shown a high percentage of changes over a period of years.

Refer to the 3-day chart tables showing exact dates when extreme high and low price has been reached and check these past dates and watch them each month in the future.

When looking up dates for Change in Trend, consider whether the market has run from any high or low price 7 to 12 days, 18 to 21, 28 to 31, 42 to 49, 57 to 65, 85 to 92, 112 to 120, 150 to 157, or 175 to 185 days. The more important the top and bottom that these Time periods start from, the more important the change.

Market Over-Balanced—The Averages or individual stocks become over-balanced after they have advanced or declined a considerable period of Time, and the greater the Time period, the greater the correction or reaction. When a Time period on a decline exceeds the Time period of a previous decline it indicates a change in trend. When the price breaks a greater number of points than the previous decline or reaction it indicates that the market is Over-Balanced and a change in trend is taking place.

Reverse this rule in a Bear Market. When stocks have been declining for a long period of Time, the first time that a rally exceeds the Time period of a previous rally it is an indication that the trend is changing, at least temporarily. The first time that the price rallies a greater number of points than a previous rally, it indicates that the Space or Price movement is Over-Balanced and a change in trend has started. The Time change is more important than reversal in price. Apply all of the rules to see if a change in trend is due at the Time when these reversals take place.

When the market is nearing the end of a long upswing or a long downswing and reaches the 3rd or 4th Section, the swings upward will be smaller in price gains and the Time period will be less than the previous Section. This is an indication that a change in trend is due. In a Bear or declining market, when the loss in points becomes less than the previous Section and the Time period is less, it is an indication that the Time cycle is running out.

Rule 9. Buy on Higher Tops and Bottoms

Buy when the market is making higher Tops and higher Bottoms which shows that the main trend is up. Sell when the market is making lower Tops and lower Bottoms which indicates the main trend is down. Time periods are always important. Check the Time period from previous Top to Top and from previous Bottom to Bottom. Also check the Time required for the market to move up from extreme low to extreme high and the Time required for prices to move down from extreme high to extreme low.

Monthly High and Low Charts—When markets are slow and narrow, and especially for low priced stocks, all you need to do is keep up the monthly high and low chart; when activity starts you can start keeping a weekly high and low chart and for stock selling at very high levels, keep the daily high and low charts, but remember that the 3-Day Swing

Chart is much more important as a Trend Indicator than a daily high and low chart.

Rule 10. Change in Trend in Bull Market

A change in trend often occurs just before or just after holidays. The following dates are important. January 3, May 30, July 4, the early part of September, after Labor Day, October 10 to 14, November 3 to 8 in election years, and November 25 to 30, Thanksgiving, and December 24 to 28. This latter period may run into the early part of January, before a definite change in trend is indicated.

When prices on the Industrial Averages or the individual stocks break the last low on a 9-Point Swing Chart or break the last low on the swing on a 3-Day Chart it is an indication that the trend is changing, at least temporarily.

Bear Market: In a declining market when prices cross the Top of the last upswing on a 9-Point Chart, or cross the top of the last upswing on a 3-Day Chart, it is the First Signal for a Change in Trend. When prices are at High Levels there are usually several swings up and down; then when the market breaks the Low of the Last Swing it indicates a reversal and change in Trend.

At low levels prices often narrow down and remain in a narrow trading range for some Time, then when they Cross the Top of the last upswing it is important for a Change in Trend.

Always check to see if the market is exactly 1, 2, 3, 4 or 5 years from any extreme High or Low price. Check back to see if the Time Period is 15, 22, 34, 42, 48 or 49 months from any extreme or low price, as these are important time periods to watch for Change in Trend.

Rule 11. Safest Buying and Selling Points

It is always safest to buy stocks after a definite Change in Trend has been established. After a stock makes bottom and has a rally, then follows the Secondary Reaction and it gets support at a higher bottom. When it starts to advance and crosses the Top of the First Rally, it is the safest Place to Buy because the market has already given an indication of uptrend. Stop Loss Orders can be placed under the Sec-ondary Bottom.

Safest Selling Point—After a market has advanced for a long time and made Final High and has the First Sharp quick Decline, then rallies and makes the Second Lower Top, and from this Top declines and Breaks the Low point of the First Decline, it is then Safer to Sell because it has given the Signal that the main Trend has changed to the Down side.

2-Day Reactions and Rallies: This is a most important time period in very fast active markets. Reactions will only run 2 days and not decline into the third day. This will happen many times before there is any indication of a Change in Trend. When a stock or the Averages react only 2 days, it is in a very strong position. You will find some of these 2-day moves shown in the table for the 3-Day Chart.

In an active, Fast Declining Market, rallies will be sharp and fast, only lasting 2 days. Study the table for the 3-Day Chart and you will find many rallies of this kind during the fall of 1929 and during 1930-31 when the big Bear Market was under way.

Remember stocks are never too High to Buy as long as the Trend is Up and they are never too Low to Sell as long as the Trend is Down; but do not overlook the fact that you must always use a Stop Loss Order for your protection. Always Go With the Trend and not against it. Buy stocks in Strong Position and Sell Stocks in Weak Positions.

Rule 12. *Price Gains in Fast Moves*

When markets are very active and advancing or declining very fast they average about 1 point per calendar day. When the Movement on Averages or individual stocks is 2 points or more per day, it is far above normal and does not last very long. Movements of this kind occur when there are

Short Time Periods and a quick corrective reaction or decline in a Bull Market. When the Trend is down in a Bear Market these quick fast rallies correct the position in a short period of time. Read the information and examples under "Short Time Periods Correct Prices."

I want to impress upon you strongly that if you expect to make a success in the stock market you must put in plenty of time studying, because the more time you put in, the more knowledge you gain, the more profits you will take out later. Over 45 years of practical experience in trying and testing rules have proven to me what is required for your success. I have given you the rules that will work; you must do your part; you must learn the rules, act on them at the right time and put them into execution.

TWENTY-FOUR NEVER-FAILING RULES

In order to make a success trading in the stock market, the trader must have definite rules and follow them. The rules given below are based upon my personal experience and anyone who follows them will make a success.

1. Amount of capital to use: Divide your capital into 10 equal parts and never risk more than one-tenth of your capital on any one trade.
2. Use stop loss orders. Always protect a trade when you make it with a stop loss order 3 to 5 points away.
3. Never overtrade. This would be violating your capital rule.
4. Never let a profit run into a loss. After you once have a profit of 3 points or more, raise your stop loss order so that you will have no loss of capital.
5. Do not buck the trend. Never buy or sell if you are not sure of the trend according to your charts.
6. When in doubt, get out, and don't get in when in doubt.
7. Trade only in active stocks. Keep out of slow, dead ones.
8. Equal distribution of risk. Trade in 4 or 5 stocks, if possible. Avoid tying up all your capital in any one stock.
9. Never limit your orders or fix a buying or selling price. Trade at the market.
10. Don't close your trades without a good reason. Follow up with a stop loss order to protect your profits.
11. Accumulate a surplus. After you have made a series of successful trades, put some money into surplus account to be used only in emergency or in times of panic.
12. Never buy just to get a dividend.
13. Never average a loss. This is one of the worst mistakes a trader can make.
14. Never get out of the market just because you have lost patience or get into the market because you are anxious from waiting.
15. Avoid taking small profits and big losses.
16. Never cancel a stop loss order after you have placed it at the time you make a trade.
17. Avoid getting in and out of the market too often.
18. Be just as willing to sell short as you are to buy. Let your object be to keep with the trend and make money.
19. Never buy just because the price of a stock is low or sell short just because the price is high.

20. Be careful about pyramiding at the wrong time. Wait until the stock is very active and has crossed Resistance Levels before buying more and until it has broken out of the zone of distribution before selling more.
21. Select the stocks with small volume of shares outstanding to pyramid on the buying side and the ones with the largest volume of stock outstanding to sell short.
22. Never hedge. If you are long of one stock and it starts to go down, do not sell another stock short to hedge it. Get out at the market; take your loss and wait for another opportunity.
23. Never change your position in the market without a good reason. When you make a trade, let it be for some good reason or according to some definite plan; then do not get out without a definite indication of a change in trend.
24. Avoid increasing your trading after a long period of success or a period of profitable trades.

When you decide to make a trade be sure that you are not violating any of these 24 rules which are vital and important to your success. When you close a trade with a loss, go over these rules and see which rule you have violated; then do not make the same mistake the second time. Experience and investigation will convince you of the value of these rules, and observation and study will lead you to a correct and practical theory for success in Wall Street.

SAFETY OF CAPITAL

Your first thought must be how to protect your capital and make your trading as safe as possible. There is one safe, sure rule, and the man who will follow it and never deviate from it will always keep his money and come out ahead at the end of every year. This rule is divide your capital into 10 equal parts and never risk more than one-tenth or 10 per cent of your capital on any one trade. If you start with $1000 you should not risk more than $100 on your first trade, and the way to limit your loss is to place a stop loss order. It is much better to have 10 shares of stock and lose 3 points or $30 than to have 100 shares and lose $300. You can always find new opportunities to make profits, so long as you have capital to operate with. Taking heavy risks in the beginning endangers your capital and impairs your judgment. Trade in such a way that you will not be disturbed mentally by a loss, if it comes.

STOP LOSS ORDERS

I feel that I cannot repeat too many times the value of using stop loss orders because it is the only safety valve to protect the investor and trader. An investor or trader will place a stop loss order and one time out of ten the stop will be caught at the exact top or bottom. After this he always remembers that and says, "If I place a stop loss order, they will just go down and catch it, or just go up and catch it and then the market will go the other way." So he does not use the stop loss order the next time. His broker often tells him that stop loss orders are always caught. The trader forgets that nine times out of ten the stop loss order was right and would have prevented big losses by getting him out at a time when the market was going against him. The one time that the stop loss order gets you out wrong it makes up for it in the next nine times that it gets you out right. So don't fail to use a stop loss order.

CHANGING YOUR MIND

A wise man changes his mind; a fool never. A wise man investigates and then decides, and a fool just decides. In Wall Street, the man who does not change his mind will soon have no change to mind. When once you have made up your mind to make a trade and you have a reason for it, do not change without a reason. The most important thing that I refer to is changing stop loss orders, or cancelling stops when the market is going against you. The first thing to do when you make a trade is to place a stop loss order, which is for your own protection. Once you have placed a stop, you have acted wisely and used good judgment. To change your mind from this decision is foolish and to cancel your stop, once you have placed it, is not based on good judgment but on hope, and hope can lead to nothing but losses in Wall Street. Nine times out of ten, when once you place a stop loss order, if you never cancel it, it will prove to be the best thing that ever happened, and the man who adheres to this rule will make a success. I reiterate, if you cannot follow a rule, do not start to speculate because you will lose all, and one of the rules that you must follow and never deviate from is to PLACE A STOP LOSS ORDER AT THE TIME YOU MAKE A TRADE AND DO NOT CANCEL IT.

OVERTRADING

History repeats because of the weakness of human nature. The greed for quick fortunes has cost the public countless millions of dollars. Every experienced stock trader knows that overtrading is his greatest weakness, but he continues to allow this weakness to be his ruin. There must be a cure for this greatest weakness in trading, and that cure is STOP LOSS ORDERS. The weakest point must be overcome, and the stop loss order is the cure for overtrading.

PROTECT YOUR PROFITS

It is just as important to protect profits as it is to protect your capital. When once you have a profit on a trade, you should never let it run into a loss. There are exceptions to this rule, and the amount of the profits should determine where stop loss orders should be placed. The following is about the safest rule that I can give you to use under average conditions. When once a stock has moved 3 points in your favor, place a stop loss order where you will be even if it is caught. In very active, high-priced stocks, it will pay you to wait until a stock shows a profit of 4 to 5 points; then move your stop loss order up to where you will have no loss should the market reverse. In this way, you will have reduced your risk to a minimum and the possibility of profits will be unlimited. As the stock moves in your favor, continue to follow up with a stop loss order, thus protecting and increasing your profits.

WHEN TO ENTER THE MARKET

It is very important to know when to buy or sell, and you must have some rule or some sign as your indication for the time to place your order to buy or sell. When you think the market is reaching bottom or top, you will find that 7 times out of 10 you will be wrong. It is not what the market does today or what you think it is going to do that is important; it is exactly what the indications are that it will do at a later date when you expect to make profits.

When a stock reaches low levels or high levels and you want to take a position, wait until it shows a sign that the trend has turned up or down. At times, you may miss the bottom or top by waiting, but you will save money by not making your trade until you have reason to believe that you are going with the trend and not against it.

One of the most important things that you should keep in mind is not how much profit or how much loss you are going to make. You should leave the money part out of the question. Your object should be to keep right on the market. Go with the trend of the market. Study all the time to determine the correct trend. Do not think about profits. If you are right on the market, the profits will come. If you are wrong, then use the old reliable protector, a stop loss order.

BUYING OR SELLING TOO SOON OR TOO LATE

Investors often get out of the market too soon, because they have held stocks for a long time, waiting for activity and higher prices, and then sell out on the first move up into new territory, which is a mistake. See Swing Charts on Atchison, American Tel. & Tel. and New York Central on page 113.

There is another type of investor who always gets out of the market too late, because when the big advance comes, he holds on and hopes that the stock will go higher than it ever does. It never reaches the price at which he wishes to sell. The first quick break comes, and he decides that if the stock advances again to its former high level, he will sell out. The stock does advance but fails to get as high, then declines still lower, and he again fixes a price in his mind at which he will sell, but this is only a "hope" price, and he sees the stock drift lower and lower until finally, in disgust, he sells out after the stock has had a big decline from the top. It is always well to wait until you can see a change in the trend before selling out, but when once you do see that the trend has changed, then sell out without delay. A good rule for this kind of a trader is to follow up with stop loss orders, even if it is 10 to 20 points away.

DELAYS DANGEROUS

Action, not delay, makes money in Wall Street. There is no use hoping, as that will not beat the game. Men who gamble on hope always go broke. You must stop hoping and start thinking. Then, after you think, unless you act at the proper time, good thinking is useless. Knowing when to act and not doing it will not help any. Delays are always dangerous. The longer you hope and delay taking action in the market, the worse your judgment gets and the surer you are to make mistakes. Stagnation is death and destruction. Action is life. Being right or wrong and not acting will never save your money or help you to make it. Remember, delays are always dangerous. It is much better to take action now than to trust to uncertain time. You should never trade when sick or depressed. Your judgment is always bad when you are below normal physically. One of the rules of a successful speculator should be to keep good health, for health is wealth.

WHEN TO PYRAMID

There are two ways of pyramiding. One is to buy more or sell more just as soon as the market breaks into new territory or makes a new high or a new low. In a fast running market, you can continue to buy or sell every 3, 5 or 10 points up or down when the market is moving in your favor, all depending on the stock or your method of pyramiding. My method is to determine the reaction levels and how many points a stock has reacted from temporary top levels or rallied from temporary bottoms. Find out whether these reactions are running 3, 5, 7, 10, or 12 points; then buy or sell your 1st, 2nd, 3rd, or 4th lot for pyramiding on reactions from the top, waiting for 3, 5, or 10 points according to the past reaction. Reverse the rule in a bear market. If you had followed this rule on General Motors from 1924 to 1929, you would find that your pyramid would have been safer than buying or selling the stock every so many points apart.

My time rule, which will help you in pyramiding, is to determine the time of the first important reaction. For example, General Motors reacted only 3 weeks from the time it started up in 1924 and was good to buy every time it reacted 2 to 3 weeks from any top, until it made the final top and the main trend turned down. Determining the time of the reactions and measuring them this way will greatly increase your profits and enable you to follow the main trend of the stock, sometimes for several years, and you can often make 100 to 200 points profit. This time rule, like other rules, works best on active high-priced stocks and should only be applied in active markets.

A pyramid should always be followed up with a stop loss order, no matter what method you use, because your profits must be protected. The more profit you have, the more room you can give the market to fluctuate, or have its reverse moves or reactions, that is, you can place your stop loss order further away from the market so that a natural reaction will not disturb your pyramid. For example, suppose you have followed a stock up and have 100 points profit on your original purchase. If the stock has had a previous reaction of 20 points, it could again react 20 points without changing the main trend, therefore your stop loss order could be 20 points under the market, because if it was caught, you would not be losing part of your capital, but only a part of your paper profits, while in the early stages of your pyramid your stop loss order would have to be closer in order to protect your original capital.

HOW MUCH PROFIT TO EXPECT

Most traders expect too large profits from the business of speculation. They do not stop to figure what a gain of 25 per cent a year means over a period of 10 to 20 years. Starting with $1000 a gain of 25 per cent per year for 10 years equals $9,313.25. $10,000 increased at the rate of 25 per cent a year amounts to $93,132.70 in 10 years. You can see how easy it is to accumulate a fortune in a reasonable length of time if one only is conservative and does not expect too much. Many traders come to Wall Street with the idea that they can double their money in a week or a month. It cannot be done. There are exceptional opportunities at times, when a large amount of money can be made in one day, one week, or one month, but these big opportunities are few and far between, and when once you have one of them and make big profits, do not let hope run away with your judgment and expect to continue to make profits right along on such an enormous scale. Remember that the market makes normal moves most of the time and that you must take normal profits the greater part of the time. Many traders buy or sell a stock without any thought of how much profit there is a possibility of them making and never think about the possibility of a loss. This should be one of your rules: Never buy or sell a stock when you don't think you can make more than 3 to 5 points' profit unless you use a stop loss order of only 1 to 2 points. It does not pay, on an average, to risk 3 to 5 points' loss for a possible gain of 3 to 5 points. Try to make a trade where you have opportunities, or at least where there is a promise of greater profits than losses. There is no use getting into a stock when you think there is only a chance of making 3 to 5 points, because you can be wrong and lose that much or more. It is better to wait until stocks cross Resistance Levels one way or the other and get in where the opportunities are for greater profits and longer swings. Scalpers do not make money; they simply get scalped. Remember that to make a success your profits must always be greater than your losses, and your rule must be to cut losses short and let your profits run.

HOW TO ANSWER A MARGIN CALL

When you make a trade and put up the required margin at the time and later the stock goes against you and the broker calls for more margin, the thing to do in most cases is not to put up more margin, but sell out at the market or buy in in case you are short. If you put up more margin, let it be on a new trade and one which you have a good reason for making when your judgment is better. Nine times out of ten after a customer puts up margin the first time, he will hold on until there is a second margin call and a third and put up as.long as he has money to put up and lose all of his capital on one trade. If the broker has to call you for margin, there is something wrong, and the best thing to do is to get out.

JOINT ACCOUNTS

Never have a joint account or trade in partnership with others if you can possibly avoid it. When two men have an account together, they may agree upon the right time to buy for long account or the right time to sell short and may be exactly right when they agree to make the trade, but here is where the hitch comes—when it comes to closing the trade they will seldom ever agree on the time and price to take profits. The result will be that they will make a mistake in getting out of the trade. One man will hold on because the other one does not want to get out and finally the market reverses and the trade goes against them; then they hold on and hope, and finally take a loss on what was a trade that they started together profitably. It is hard for one mind to work on the stock market and keep right, but it is much harder for two to agree and work in the market. The only way that two could make a success with it would be for one to do the buying and selling and the other to do nothing but place the stop loss orders. Stop loss orders will protect both of them when they make mistakes. It is a bad rule for a man and his wife to have a joint account together. The action of getting in and out of the market should be up to one man, who should learn to act and act quickly and not be influenced by a partner in a speculative deal.

WHAT TRADERS DON'T WANT TO KNOW

The average trader does not want to hear a painful truth. They want something in accordance with what they hope for. When they buy a stock they believe all the news, rumors, views and lies that are bullish, but just let some report come out that is bad or let someone tell him something unfavorable about the stock he has bought and he refuses to believe it. It is the truth that will help him and truth that he should want to hear, not something that will build up his hopes and cause him losses later. A trader after he has made a mistake, says "I am going to do different next time," but he doesn't and that is why we always have old lambs in Wall Street to lead the young lambs down the same lane to losses that the old lambs have followed. Real inside truth about losses in Wall Street is seldom ever told. Traders, big and little, always talk about their profits and brag about their successful trades, but keep quiet about their losses. Therefore, the innocent lamb, when he comes to Wall Street, is led to believe that there is nothing but profits to be made, instead of hearing the other side of the story of how losses are made in Wall Street, which is a thing that would really help him and prevent him from making the same mistake. The new lamb should know that failing to place a stop loss order and overtrading have been the cause of over 90 per cent of the failures in Wall Street. Therefore, in order to make a success he must act in a way to overcome the weak points which have caused the ruin of others.

HUMAN ELEMENT THE GREATEST WEAKNESS

When a trader makes a profit, he gives himself credit and feels that his judgment is good and that he did it all himself. When he makes losses, he takes a different attitude and seldom ever blames himself or tries to find the cause with himself for the losses. He finds excuses; reasons with himself that the unexpected happened, and that if he had not listened to some one else's advice, he would have made a profit. He finds a lot of ifs, ands, and buts, which he imagines were no fault of his. This is why he makes mistakes and losses the second time.

The investor and trader must work out his own salvation and blame himself and no one else for his losses, for unless he does, he will never be able to correct his weaknesses. After all, it is your own acts that cause your losses, because you did the buying and the selling. You must look for the trouble within and correct it. Then you will make a success, and not before.

One of the main reasons why traders make losses is because they do not think for themselves and allow others to think for them and advise them, whose advice and judgment is no better than their own. To make a success, you must study and investigate for yourself. Unless you change from a "lamb" to a thinker and seek knowledge, you will go the way of all lambs,—to slaughter under the margin caller's axe. Others can only help you when you help yourself, or show you how to help yourself.

I can give you the best rules in the world and the best methods for determining the position of a stock, and then you can lose money on account of the human element which is your greatest weakness. You will fail to follow rules. You will work on hope or fear instead of facts. You will delay. You will become impatient. You will act too quickly or you will delay too long in acting, thus cheating yourself on account of your human weakness and then blaming it on the market. Always remember that it is your mistake that causes losses and not the action of the market or the manipulators. Therefore, strive to follow rules, or keep out of speculation for you are doomed to failure.

CHAPTER III

HOW TO SELECT INDEPENDENT MOVERS

Many stocks make new Highs while other stocks are making new Lows and start moves independent of the Averages and the different groups of stocks. You can determine when these independent moves start by studying the action on the chart for several years back.

For example—Cities Service. 1938 High 11. 1939 Low 4. 1942 Low 2, High 3½. The stock had held in a range between 11 and 2 for four years and during 1942 made a range of only 1½ points per share, indicating that it was thoroughly liquidated and no one but the insiders wanted to buy it. You could have taken a chance and bought the stock at this time because you could not lose but two or three dollars per share if it went off the board. But what you want to know is when to buy, when it is safe, and when it shows a definite Up-Trend. In 1943 the stock crossed 11, the 1938 High, after a period of five years which indicated much higher prices, and you should have bought it at once. It continued to make Higher Bottoms and Higher Tops, showing the main Trend Up.

1948, June High 64½. The stock had advanced 53 points after it showed main Trend Up. When you bought it at 11, a 3 point Stop Loss Order would have held it and you could have doubled your money four or five times without pyramiding.

1949, High 48. 1949, Low 38, which is still above the 1948 levels. As long as the stock can hold above 38 it is still in position to go higher as the earnings are good.

Buying One Stock and Selling Another Short

I have stated before under "Cross Currents of the Market" that some stocks advance and make new Highs while others decline and make new Lows. There are many times when you can sell one stock short at a High Level and buy another stock that is selling at a Low Level and the prices of these stocks will come together and you will make profits on both.

Radio and Pepsi-Cola

1947, August 34½, for Pepsi-Cola. It had previously sold at 40 and was making Lower Tops and on all the rules the Trend was down. Suppose you sold short 100 shares of Pepsi-Cola at 32. At the same time Radio was selling at 8, showing good support around Low Levels. You bought 100 shares of Radio at 8 and placed a Stop Loss Order on it at 7. On the Pepsi-Cola short you would place a Stop Loss Order at 35, making a total risk of about $400 plus commissions if both Stops were caught. They were not. Pepsi-Cola continued to decline and Radio advanced.

1947 Low on Radio 7½. Using my rule of a 100% advance we would watch Radio at 15 for Top. 1948, June High, 15 up 100% and the volume of trading was very heavy and the stock failed to go through. You had plenty of time to sell it around 15.

In 1948, Pepsi-Cola was selling below 20, which was a 50% decline from the last highest selling price, 40½. Having broken this important support level you would remain short of Pepsi-Cola reducing Stop Loss Order to 21. 1948, December, Pepsi-Cola Low 7½, down to the 1939 Low Level where it received support. This would be the time to cover short Pepsi-Cola at 8. This would give you 24 points profit on Pepsi-Cola and approximately 7 points on Radio. Pepsi-Cola did not decline to 7 and advanced to 12. You could have bought it with a Stop at 7 which would not have been caught.

When to Buy Radio

Look up the chart for the High and Low in recent years. 1945, High 19⅝; 1947, Low 7½. 1948 High 15. The 50% point or half-way between 7½ and 15 is 11¼. The last extreme high was 19⅝, 50% of this high selling price would be 9.81 or approximately $10.00 per share. 1949, June 14, Radio declined to 9¾ and around June 29 was still selling as low as 9⅝, giving you an opportunity to buy all the stock you wanted at $10.00 per share. You could place a Stop-Loss Order at 8½. The next thing you want to know is: When will it show strong Up Trend. When it crosses 11¼ and closes above this level it will indicate higher. The next objective is the 1949 High of 15 and the 1945 High at 19⅝. Should Radio ever cross 20 it will then be in a very strong position and indicate very much higher prices. I belive in the future of Radio; it has great possibilities, and may again become a real leader in the future.

CHAPTER IV

PERCENTAGE OF HIGH AND LOW PRICES

One of the greatest discoveries I ever made was how to figure the percentage of high and low prices on the averages and individual stocks. The percentages of extreme high and low levels indicate future resistance levels.

There is a relation between every low price to some future high price and a percentage of the low price indicates what levels to expect the next high price. At this price you can sell out long stocks and sell short with a limited risk.

The extreme high price or any minor tops are related to future bottoms or low levels. The percentage of the high price tells where to expect low prices in the future and gives you resistance levels where you can buy with a limited risk.

The most important resistance level is 50% of any high or low price. Second in importance is 100% on the lowest selling price on the averages or individual stocks. You must also use 200%, 300%, 400%, 500%, 600% or more, depending upon the price and the Time Periods from High and Low. Third in importance is 25% of the Lowest price or the Highest price. Fourth in importance is 12½% of the extreme Low or extreme High price. Fifth in importance is 6¼% of the Highest price, but this is only to be used when the averages or individual stocks are selling at very high levels.

Sixth in importance is 33 1/3 and 66 2/3%. These percentages should be calculated and watched for resistance next after 25% and after 50%.

You should always have percentage tables made up on the Industrial Averages and on the individual stocks you trade in in order to know where these important resistance levels are located.

1896, August 8, low 28.50 for the 12 Industrial Averages. This was the extreme Low price and the percentage on this price is very important.

1896, Aug. 8, low 28.50	1921, Aug. 24, low 64
50% is 42.75	25% is 80.00
100% is 57.00	50% is 96.00
200% is 85.50	62½% is 104.00
300% is 114.00	75% is 112.00
400% is 142.50	100% is 128.00
450% is 156.75	125% is 144.00
500% is 171.00	137½% is 152.00
550% is 185.50	150% is 160.00
575% is 192.75	162½% is 168.00
600% is 199.50	175% is 176.00
700% is 228.00	187½% is 184.00
800% is 256.50	200% is 192.00
900% is 285.00	212½% is 200.00
1000% is 313.50	225% is 208.00
1100% is 342.00	237½% is 216.00
1200% is 370.50	250% is 224.00
1250% is 384.75	275% is 240.00
	300% is 256.00
	400% is 320.00
	500% is 384.00

1932, July 8, low 40.56 for the 30 Industrial Averages. The percentages are as follows:

1932, July 8, low 40.56	1942, April 28, low 92.69
25% is 50.70	12½% is 104.27
50% is 60.84	25% is 115.86
75% is 70.98	37½% is 127.44
100% is 81.12	50% is 139.00
150% is 101.40	62½% is 150.58
175% is 111.54	75% is 162.16
200% is 121.68	100% is 185.38
225% is 131.82	112½% is 196.96
250% is 141.96	125% is 208.45

—31—

275% is 152.10
300% is 162.24
325% is 172.38
350% is 182.56
375% is 192.66
400% is 202.80
425% is 212.94
1933, July 18, low 84.45
100% is 168.90
1933, Oct. 21, low 82.20
100% is 164.40
1934, July 26, low 84.58
100% is 169.16
1938, March 31, low 97.50
100% is 195.00

PERCENTAGE OF HIGH
PRICES
1919, Nov. 3, high 119.62
100%   is 239.24
200%   is 358.86
325%   is 388.50
1929, Sept. 3, high 386.10
50%   is 193.05
75%   is 96.52
87½% is 48.32
1930, April 16, high 296.35
50%   is 148.17
75%   is 74.08
87½% is 37.04
1933, July 18, high 110.53
25% from this is 82.90

1937, March 8, high 195.50
50% is 97.75
1943, July 15, high 146.50
50% is 73.25
25% on this price is 183.27
50% on this price is 219.75
1946, May 29, last extreme high 213.36
25% off of this price is 160.02

Other percentages for resistance levels of this price can be calculated.

Stocks Selling Below 50 Per Cent Level

It is very important when a stock breaks 50% or one-half between the extreme high and extreme low level. When it does not get support and holds at this level, it is in a very weak position and indicates a decline to 75% down or more between extreme high and extreme low.

Fifty per cent of the highest selling price is of still greater importance. When a stock breaks this level it is in a very weak position because if it is going to get support and advance it will get it when the stock has declined 50% from the highest level. Do not buy stocks after they get below this level until you see an indication of support based on all of the rules.

Market Action Proves the Rules

After we have calculated the percentage on the extreme low prices and on the extreme high prices it is important to calculate the 50% or half-way point between the extreme low and extreme high prices.
Examples:

1896, Low 28.50 to 1919, High 119.62 gives the half-way point at 74.06. 28.50 low to extreme high in 1929 of 386.10 gives 50% or half-way point of 207.28. 1921, Low 64 to 386 high gives the 50% or half-way point of 225.00. 1930, high, 296.25, to the low of 64 gives the 50% or half-way point at 180.12. 28.50 low to 296.25 high gives the 50% or half-way point at 162.37. 1937 high 195.50 to 28.50 low gives the 50% or half-way point at 112. 1937 high 195.50 to 1938 low 97.50 gives the 50% or half-way point at 146.50. 1932 low 40.56 to 1946 high 213.36 gives the half-way point at 126.96. 1942 low 92.69 to 1946 high 213.36 gives the fifty per cent or half-way point at 153.02.

When all of these figures are completed for resistance levels we proceed to prove that they work in calling tops and bottoms. Up to 1919 the extreme high on the Dow-Jones 30 Industrial Averages was 119.62. After 1921 the price was moving up from the low of 64 and we find that 87½% on 64 gives 120.00, making the old top and this resistance level very important. When prices cross the extreme High level we look in the table of percentages above 64 to see the resistance levels indicated for tops. We find that 500% gives 384.00. On September 3, 1929, the Averages made high at 386.10. Looking over the table of percentages from 28.50 low we see that 1250% is 384.75. Next figuring the important percentages on the old high price of 119.62 we find that 225% added to 119.62 gives 388.50 which shows three resistance levels at 384.00, 384.75 and 388.50. The Averages made extreme High at 386.10 but the highest closing price was 381.10. The Three-Day Chart and the 9-Point Swing Chart both showed the market was Top at these important resistance levels.

After the extreme High was reached the next point is to figure where the important resistance level and buying level should be. Rule 3 says that 50% of the highest selling price is the most important. 50% of 386.10 gives 193.00 as a support and buying level. The fastest decline in history followed the high in September, 1929, running to November 13, low 195.35, holding $2\frac{1}{2}$ points above the important support level making this a buying level. Because the market failed to reach the exact 50% point it showed greater strength. We next apply the same rule and add 50% to the low of 195.35 and this gives 293.02 as a possible rally point and selling level.

April 16, 1930, high 297.25, a little over 3 points above the important resistance level, but prices did not go five points above it, based on Rule 2 that it requires five points above a resistance level or 5 points below an Old Bottom or resistance level to indicate a definite change in Trend.

After this top was established and the Trend turned down, based on the 3-Day Chart and the 9-Point Swing Chart, we next figure the 50% or half-way point between the low of 195.35 and the high of 297.25. This gives 246.30. When this point was broken it indicated much lower prices and you will note that the last rally, on September 10, 1930, made high at 247.21, just above this important 50% point. Later when the low of November 13, of 195.35 was broken and the averages broke 193, the 50% point of 386.10 they were in a very weak position and indicated much lower prices. The decline continued subject to normal rallies until July 8, 1932, when extreme Low was reached at 40.56. If we take $87\frac{1}{2}\%$ from 386.10 we get 48.26. If we look at the table from the extreme Low of 28.50 we find 50% gives 42.75 as resistance level. If we subtract $37\frac{1}{2}\%$ from the 1921 low of 64.00 we get 40.00 as a support level. Going back to 1897, April 8, the high was 40.37 and on the 3-Day Chart this level was crossed on June 4, 1897, which turned the main trend up and the Averages never sold at that level again until July 8, 1932, when they made bottom at 40.56.

From the extreme Low of 40.56 we calculate where the first resistance level should be met. We add 100% to this low level and it gives 81.12.

On September 8, 1932, the Averages rallied to 81.50, making top exactly on this important 50% point.

1933, February 27, low 49.68. This was the low of the secondary decline. You will notice in the table that 25% on 40.56 gives 50.70 making this a very important support level and the Averages made Bottom just one point below this level. The upward Trend was resumed.

1933, July 18, high 110.53. Why did the Averages make Top at this level? 175% on 40.56 gives 111.54 as an important resistance level and 112.00 is 75% on 64 low, making this an important resistance level and a place to sell as the volume of sales and Time Periods indicated top for a reaction because it was one year from the low in July, 1932.

We apply the same rules to the high of 110.53 and subtract 25% from this high selling price and it gives 82.90 as a support and buying level. The market had one of the fastest declines in history for a period of three days, July 21, low 84.45, holding just above this important support level. A rally followed and if you bought stocks at this time you could have sold them when the Averages rallied back to 107.00.

1933, October 21, last extreme low 82.20, less than 1 point under the support level of 82.90. This extreme Low level was the last time the Averages sold that low until the time of this writing, June 30, 1949. It is important to figure 100% on 82.20 which gives 164.40 as an important resistance level.

1934, July 26, low 84.58. This was the third time around this low level and it indicated a big Bull Market to follow because prices had held above 100% on the low of 40.56. A big Bull Market followed and prices continued to work up until they crossed 110.53, the high of July, 1933. After crossing this high level what price should we figure the Averages to go to? We know that 50% of 386.10 is 193.05. We know that the Old Bottom of November, 1929, was 195.35 and we know that the Averages made top February 24, 1931, at 196.96; therefore, the logical resistance and selling level would be 193-195.

1937, March 8, high 195.50, at the important 50% point and at the Old Tops and Bottoms, the 3-Day Chart and the 9-Point Swing Chart confirmed that this was Final High. We wish to figure the logical point for the next decline. We apply the same rule and subtract 50% from 195.50 which gives 97.75 as a support and buying level.

1938, March 31, the Averages made low at 97.50 and another Bull Market started.

1938, November 10, high 158.75. This was 62½% on the last low. The main Trend turned down from this level and the Averages broke the important 50% point and continued on down, making lower tops and lower bottoms on the important swings and finally breaking back below 110 and breaking 97.50.

1942, April 28, low 92.69. This was less than 5 points under the low of 1938 and was a buying point as this was a Triple Bottom, which was confirmed by the 3-Day Chart and the 9-Point Swing Chart. It was the place to buy stocks for a big Bull Market. From this low level we figured the percentages on 92.69. 50% on this is 139. 12½% the first important resistance level was 104.27.

1942, August 7, last extreme low 104.58. Just above this important support level at 104.27 from 213.33 to 104.27 the 50% point is 158.80.

Next we figure the important resistance levels from which the Averages should react. 50% between 92.69 and 195.50 is 144.09. 50% between 1937 high of 195.50 and 1938 low 97.50 gives 146.50.

1943, July 15, high 146.50, exactly at these important resistance levels where top was indicated for reaction. The Time Period running out in July also called for top and a reaction just the same as it did in July, 1933. The Averages reacted but did not break back far enough to show that the main Trend had turned down. Note that 37½% on 92.69

gives 127.44, which level was never broken. 1943, November 30 last low 128.94. Later when the Averages advanced and crossed 146.50 the old top and important resistance level, they indicated the next top at 158.75 made November 10, 1938. When the Averages crossed this level they again indicated the most important 50% point at 193-195.

After the war ended in August, 1945, the averages had made a last low on July 27th of 159.95; having already crossed the old tops they indicated much higher prices. The advance continued and the averages finally crossed 195.50 indicating higher prices. The first important percentage resistance level was 207.50 which was 50% between 28.50 and 386.10. The averages made top at this level, February 4, 1946, and had a quick reaction to 184.04 on February 26, later crossing 208.00. The next and most important resistance level was the 50% point between the extreme High of 386.10 and the extreme Low of 40.56. This was 213.33 and on May 29, 1946, the Averages made high at 213.36 exactly on this important 50% point. Note also that 425% on 40.56 was 212.94 making this a doubly important resistance level.

From the high of 213.36 we subtract 25% to get the first resistance level and buying point which gives 160.03.

October 30, 1946, extreme low, 160.49, again May 19, 1947, low 161.32, June 14, 1949, low 160.62. This was three times the market made bottom at this important support level and prices were holding above July 27, 1945, when the last low was 159.95.

From these strong support levels the Averages made a higher bottom on February 11, 1948, and advanced to 194.49 on June 14, 1948. This was back to the old 50% selling level where Old Bottoms and Tops had occurred so many times, making this a selling level which was confirmed by the 3-Day Chart and the 9-Point Swing Chart.

Present Position of the Dow-Jones 30 Industrial Averages

They have received support for the third time at 25% down from 213.36 and the last Old Bottom of July 27, 1945, is at 159.95. Should the Averages break these levels and close under them it will indicate 152.00 which is 275% on 40.56 and the next resistance point is 146.50 the Old Top and important 50% point.

1942 low 92.69, 1946 high 213.36, 50% or ½ point is 153.02.

At the time of this writing, July 19th, 1949, the averages have crossed 175 and indicate 177½, a resistance level, because it is 50% of the range between 160.49 and 194.49; therefore, from around 177½ there could be a moderate reaction, and when the averages cross 182½, the high of January 7, 1949, they will indicate much higher prices.

When the averages reach important resistance levels, or advance to old tops or decline to old low levels, you should study the position of the individual stocks you trade in and apply all of the rules given to these individual stocks.

Let the Market Tell Its Own Story

When you start to study the stock market do not have any fixed ideas and do not BUY or SELL on HOPE or FEAR. Learn the three most important factors, TIME, PRICE and VOLUME OF SALES. Study my rules and apply them. Be ready to change quickly when the rules show that the market is making a change in TREND. Let the action of the market tell its own story and trade only on definite indications based on the rules and you will make profits.

CHAPTER V

TIME PERIODS OF SHORT DURATION CORRECT PRICES

You often hear people say the market needs a correction. Prices have advanced too fast or declined too fast. When this happens in an advancing market it becomes overbought, shorts have covered and the technical position of the market is weakened, therefore, a price correction is in order. This may be a sharp, quick decline in a very short period of time. The fact that the price declines very fast scares people, they lose hope and decide the market is going very much lower, when as a matter of fact a *short decline* in a very *short period* of *time* has corrected the technical position from a weak position to a strong one.

The same occurs when the market has been declining for some time and it has built up an over extended short interest and longs have liquidated leaving the market in a weak technical position. Then a sharp advance takes place on short covering in a very short period of time. This causes buyers to become over confident and buy at the top and decide that the movement is going to continue but the technical position has been weakened and the market has been corrected on the short side by this sharp rally. Then the main Trend continues on down.

Apply all of the rules at all times in order to prevent misjudging the Trend of the market or making mistakes. Remember, when you do make a mistake or see that you are wrong, the way to correct it is to get out of the market immediately, or best of all when you make trade, place a Stop Loss Order for the protection of your capital. Keep in mind at all times the greatest TIME PERIOD, or the greatest correction of the market when it is advancing, and when a market is declining keep in mind at all times the greatest TIME PERIOD that had occurred when the market had rallied in a Bear Market. Keeping up with these Time Periods will help you to determine the Trend of the market. That is why I am reviewing these market movements and pointing out the Time Periods which have brought about sharp, quick rallies or sharp, quick declines and ended the market movement for that period of time. The main Trend as outlined before continues. All of the prices referred to are the Dow-Jones 30 Industrial Averages.

The New York Stock Exchange closed on July 30, 1914, due to the outbreak of war and heavy selling. It did not open until December the 12th, 1914, when heavy liquidation carried prices to the Lowest Level of many years.

1914, December 24, low 53.17. From this Low Level the market continued to advance as we were in a war period with large orders and corporations were accumulating large profits. This Bull Market continued for about one year after the end of the World War, November 11, 1918.

1919, November 3. High 119.62 for the Dow-Jones 30 Industrial Averages. This was the highest price in history up to that time, and they had advanced from 53.17, an advance of 66.45 points. Therefore, when a sharp, quick decline occurred after November 3, 1919, especially after the market had been advancing for nearly five years, you would know this was a SIGNAL that the Final Top had been reached and the Trend was turning down. The Trend continued down subject to normal rallies until August 24, 1921, low 63.90; this decline lasted nearly 22 months. From the 1921 low, the main Trend continued up to March 20, 1923, high 105.50, an advance of 19 months. From this Top Level there was a down swing until October 27, 1923 low, 85.50. A decline of 20 points in seven months time. This was a normal, natural decline. Refer to 9 Point Swing Chart which says that the declines and advances run in 20, 30, 40 points and so forth. But 20 points is an average move in the normal market. Therefore, this would be a point to check on all the charts, especially the Three-Day Chart, and watch for Change of Trend. Watch for the first sharp, quick decline that made a correction and indicated the trend would continue up.

1924, February 6, high 101.50. An advance of 16 points from the last low, and prices had not yet crossed the top of March 20, 1923, which would be a SIGNAL for higher prices.

May 14, low 88.75. This was higher by more than 3 points above the low of October 27, 1923, indicating a better support and higher prices. The time for this decline was 69 days. Refer to Rule 8 TIME PERIODS which says market movements often run from 60 to 72 days.

1925, March 6, high 123.50. This price crossed the 1919 high by nearly 4 points. Our rule says that prices have to go five points or more into new High to give a definite indication that the market is going to continue up. However, this was the first indication that prices were going higher. But a corrective reaction was in order as the market had been advancing from the last extreme Low of 85.50.

1925, March 30, low 115, down 8½ points, not 10 points which was a normal reaction and indication of strength. Also the fact that the Averages did not go 5 points below the high of 1919 which was 119.62 was another good indication that they were going higher, and that this correction which lasted only 24 days was only a minor reaction in a Bull Market.

1926, February 11, high 162.50, up 47.50 from the last Low of 115. Time period 355 days and time for a corrective reaction.

1926, March 30, low 135.25. Down 37.25. Time 17 days. This was a rapid decline moving down much faster than one point per calendar day and was the proper correction of a Bull Market and the trend continued up.

1927, October 3, high 199.78, an advance of 60.25 in 186 days. The fact that the Averages were just below 200, and Rule 3 says that at 100, 200 and 300 and all even figures there is always public selling and some resistance. This indicated there should be a corrective reaction and it did come in a short period of time.

1927, October 22, low 179.78, down 20 points in 119

days. This was a correction and an advance followed. Later prices crossed 200, which was an indication of higher prices as they were in a new High territory.

1928, November 28, high 299.35, up 119.50 points in 403 days, with the price just under the 300 level a resistance and Selling Level, where a corrective reaction should occur, especially after more than one year's time had elapsed from the previous Bottom.

1928, December 10, low 254.50, down 44 points in 12 days. This was one of the sharpest corrective reactions that ever occurred since the Bull Campaign started in August, 1921. In fact, the prices did not go lower after this sharp, quick decline, but started making Higher Bottoms, an indication that it was all over and that prices were going higher.

1929, March 1; high 324.50, up 70 points in 81 days. This price was close to 325, an even figure at which the public always sells, and a corrective reaction was again in order.

1929, March 26, low 281, down 43½ points in 25 days. Note this was almost the same decline that occurred between November 28, 1928, and December 10, 1928. The market received support at these Levels with the same price decline and an advance was resumed.

1929, May 6, high 331, up 50 points in 41 days. The market had now made a new High which was an indication that after a reaction it would go higher.

May 31, low 291, down 41 points in 25 days, the same time period as the previous reaction, but making a Bottom 10 points higher than the previous Bottom, an indication of good support and that the main Trend was up, and that it would continue to be up.

1929, September 3, high 386.10, up 95 points in 95 days. (One of our rules is that a fast advancing market will gain about one point per calendar day.) This proved to be final High for the greatest Bull Market which had gone up on the greatest volume in history with the greatest public buying. In fact, public buying occurred from all over the world and had been greatly overdone, and it was only natural after the market had been advancing from August, 1921, to September, 1929, a period of a little over 8 years, and with prices up from 64 to 386.10, it was time to watch for a SIGNAL of the end. And it came, suddenly and unexpectedly! Here is the place to study the 3-Day Chart and you will see where the first SIGNAL was given on this chart. The public was heavily loaded with stocks, shorts had covered, and when the public started to sell, there were no buyers and a wide open break occurred.

1929, November 13, low 195.50, a decline of 190.60 points in 71 days, the greatest decline in the shortest period of time in history. This was the corrective decline from an over bought market in a short period of time, and a natural rally which always occurs after the first sharp decline was in order. The SECONDARY RALLY always occurs after a prolonged advance and a sharp decline. Then, in a Bear Market, after a sharp decline, there is first a sharp rally and a SECONDARY DECLINE which marks final Bottom and the main Trend turns up.

1929, December 9, high 267, up 71½ points in 27 days. This was a sharp advance from an oversold condition on short covering and a natural, quick reaction was in order.

1929, December 20, low 227, down 40 points in 11 days. This decline was too rapid and the rally was in order.

1930, April 16, high 297¼, up 102 points from the low of November 13 in 154 days' time. This was the SECONDARY RALLY in a big Bear Market which always occurs after an advance of this kind. Watch for the first SIGNAL of a sharp decline to indicate the rally was over and go short. Looking at the 3-Day Chart, you will see how it gave the SIGNAL that the advance was over and prices continued toward lower Levels subject to small reactions until 1930, October 22, low 181.50, a decline of 116¼ points in 188 days. The fact that prices broke below the low of November 13, 1929, was an indication that the Bear Market was going to continue, and that there would be nothing but sharp, quick rallies when the market became oversold, as it had at this time.

1930, October 28, high 198.50, up 17 points in 16 days. One of our rules that normal rallies will run around 20 points. The fact that this advance failed to reach 20 points in 6 days indicated the market was in a weak position, and would go lower, which it did.

1930, November 10, low 168.50, down 30 points in 13 days. This was a very rapid decline because a liquidation was increasing as prices worked lower. However, from all sharp declines quick rallies lasting only a short period of time must occur.

1930, November 25, high 191.50, up 33 points in 15 days' time. This was a sharp quick rally and prices were moving up too fast. And the fact that prices did not reach the old low of November 13, 1929, which was 195.50, was an indication of weakness and lower prices. Also the fact that they were below the high of October 28, 1930, of 198.50, another indication that the main trend was still down, and this was only a short rally in the Bear Market.

LIQUIDATION AFTER A PROLONGED DECLINE AND A SHARP RALLY IN A BEAR MARKET

1930, December 2, high 187.50. From this lower top the decline started, and it was very severe in this final wave of liquidation as the public had held on and hoped for a Bull Market which did not come.

December 17, low 154.50, down 33 points in 15 days. This was a decline of almost 2 points per calendar day which was much more rapid than a normal decline should be, and near old support levels and above 150, a natural point for support for a rally to follow.

1931, February 24, high 196.75. Note that this was near the old bottom of November 13, 1929, and was under the high of October 28, 1930, making it a natural resistance and selling Level based on our rules that Bottoms become Tops and Tops become Bottoms and when these old Levels are reached, selling or buying takes place. The time period from December 17, 1930, was 69 days. This compares with 71 days, the decline from September 3, 1929, to November

13, again confirming Rule 8 of 67 to 72 day Time Periods. At the Top, February 24, 1931, the price was up 42¼ points and below December 17, 1930. This sharp quick rally in the Bear Market soon died out. By reviewing and studying the three-day chart you can see how the indication was given for lower prices again caused by reviewing all of the starting points and main Tops which move started all the way down from 1929. Each Top had been lower and Bottoms were continuing to be lower. Therefore, the main Trend was still down.

1931, June 2, low 119.60. This was down to the old high of 1919. According to the Rules, a rally should always take place as old Bottoms become Tops and old Tops become Bottoms. Therefore, we would expect a rally from this level as the price was down 77¼ points from the high of February 24, 1931, in a Time Period of 98 days.

1931, June 27, high 157.50, an advance of 37.90 points in 25 days. This price was up just above the old Bottom of December 17, 1930, but went only 3 points above it, and not 5 according to the rules. Therefore, this would be a selling Level, especially as the advance had been in such a short period of time.

1931, October 5, low 85½, down 72 points in 100 days, almost the same time period as the previous one.

1931, November 9, high 119.50. Back to the low of June 2, 1931, and to the old Top of 1919, making this a selling Level. The time of this rally was 35 days, and the advance was 34 points. Rule 12 states that a fast advance runs about 1 point per calendar day. Therefore, again you should go short on this rally, and by watching the three-day chart you would get a SIGNAL that the Trend was turning down again.

1932, February 10, low 70. The time of this fast decline was 92 days. Price decline 49½ points.

1932, February 19, high 89½, up 19½ points in 9 days. This was four points above the Low of October 5, 1931, and a selling Level. The market slowed down and met resistance near this Level, and the three-day chart indicated that the market had made Top for another decline.

Final Liquidation in Great Bear Market

1932, March 9, high 89½, the same high as of the 19th of February. Time, 18 days from the last high, meeting resistance at this same high of February 19th indicated lower prices unless the Averages could close above these levels, which they did not.

1932, July 8, low 40.56, down 49 points in 121 days. During the period from March 9, 1932, to July 8, 1932, the greatest rally was 7½ and 8 points, not making as much as 10 points, which is the smallest normal rally based on our rules. None of these rallies lasted more than 1, 3, 4, 4 and 7 days. The last 7-day rally from June 9 low, 44½, to June 16 high 51½, was 7 days with a gain of only 7 points.

After the low of July 8, the first rally lasted 8 days, and the price was up 5 points. Then a reaction of three days and the market only declined two points on Averages. Following this there was a rapid advance with only 3 and 5 day reactions until September 8, 1932, high 81.50, up 41 points, time 62 days. This was an advance on percentage of 100 per cent on the Averages. Refer to Rule 8 which states that these SECONDARY DECLINES or advances last 60 to 67 days.

From the last high of April 16, 1930, the greatest time on rallies was 69 days. Most of them were 25, 35 and 45 days, which were the great rallies in a Bear Market.

From November 13, 1929, to April 16, 1930, the time was 154 days, the price advance was 101.25.

1932, September 8, high 81½. A sharp reaction followed. October 10, low 57½, down 24 points in 32 days. This was a corrective reaction and a moderate rally followed.

Secondary Decline After September 8 High

1933, February 27, low 49.50, down 32 points, time 172 days. Compares with the Secondary Time Period of 154 days in April 16, 1930. After this SECONDARY DECLINE,

President Roosevelt was inaugurated for the first time and closed all the banks. After the banks reopened, everything started to advance. Later we went off of the gold standard which was inflationary, and the prices of stocks continued to advance in very large volume indicating up trend and a Bull Market. After these SECONDARY DECLINES, which correct the technical position of the market, the advance which follows is nearly always more rapid and greater than the first advance which started from the Bottom when the main Trend first turned up.

1933, July 18, high 110.50, up 61 points, time 144 days from February 27 low. This was on greatly increased volume and the market became over bought. At this time Dr. E. A. Crawford failed. He was one of the largest speculators in grains and other commodities, and was also heavily long of stocks. The heavy selling in commodities after Dr. Crawford's failure started liquidation in stocks and brought about the most severe decline in a short period of three days' time that had occurred since 1929. This was a sharp corrective reaction in a short period of time.

July 21, low 84.45, down 26.08 points in three days. The price was still above the high level of September 8, 1932, indicating good support and a buying level for a rally after such a sharp severe decline on heavy liquidation.

Secondary Rally

After the stock market makes Top and has the first sharp decline, there is always a SECONDARY RALLY that carries prices up around the extreme high Level, and if this rally is considerably lower than the first extreme Top, it is an indication of greater weakness.

1933, September 18, high 107.68, up 23.23 points in 62 days. This price was 3 points below the high of July 18, and the three-day chart soon showed a reversal and the Trend turned down again.

1933, October 9, high 100½. October 21 low 82.20, a decline of 18¼ points in 12 days. This was a quick, sharp decline in a short period of time, and the decline did not run

20 points which was an indication of good support. This was the lowest Level that the averages sold from 1933 up to 1949. In fact, this was the beginning of another upswing of a Bull Market, and the time period from July 18, 1933, high to October 21 low was 95 days. Refer to Rule 8 which says that advances and declines often run 90 to 98 days.

Sharp, Corrective Declines

1934, April 20, high 107.50. This was below the 1933 and 1934 tops.

1934, May 14, low 89.50, down 18 points, time 24 days. The fact that the market again declined only about the same as it did October 21, 1933, not going down 20 points, was an indication prices were getting support and were going higher.

Final Low

1934, July 11, high 99½.

1934, July 26, low 84½, down 15 points in 15 days. Rule 12 says that a sharp decline often runs about one point per day, and as prices were low below $100.00 per share this was a normal market and a normal decline. The decline had run a little over one year from the high on July 18, 1933, and it was time for a Change in Trend. By studying the three-day chart you can see how it indicated the market had made Bottom and that by crossing three-day Tops the Trend had turned up. In fact, the last important Top was July 11, 99½, and crossing 100 is always an indication for higher prices.

July 26, 1934, was the starting of another big Bull Market, and the fact that the price held two points above the low of October 21, 1933, showed it was a continuation of the Bull Market which started in 1932.

1935, February 18, high 108½, just one point above the Top of April 20, 1934, and the resistance or selling Level.

1935, March 18, low 96, down 12½ points in 28 days. This was a normal reaction running a little over 10 points and indicated support and an advance to follow.

1936, April 6, high 163.25. This was up a little over one year from the low of March 18, 1935, and was time for a corrective reaction.

1936, April 30, low 141.50, down 21¾ points in 24 days. The market received support here and showed an up trend on the three-day chart. The fact that the decline ran only a little over 20 points indicated that it was a normal re-action in a Bull Market.

1936, August 10, high 170.50, again high enough for a corrective reaction.

August 21, low 160.50, down 10 points in 11 days' time. This was only a normal reaction, and it was time to buy stocks as the main Trend was still up.

Final High in the Bull Market

1937, March 10, high 195.50. This was up to the old Lows made in November, 1929, and just under the old Top Levels. A natural resistance level and selling point for the market to make final high. The Bull Market was started July 8, 1932, and resulted in an advance of 155 points in 56 months' time. The starting of the last leg of the Bull Market was July 26, 1934, to March 10, 1937. This was 31 months and 12 days, and the advance was 110 points. The decline started after March 10 and, based on the three-day chart and all of the rules, indications were plain that the market had made final Top, and that the main Trend had turned down. However, we always know that the SECOND-ARY RALLY must come after final Top is reached.

Secondary Rally in Bear Market

1937, June 14, low 163.75, down 32¾ points, time from March 10, 96 days, a normal Time Period based on Rule 8, and time for the SECONDARY RALLY to take place.

August 14, 1937, high 190.50, up 26¾ points in 61 days. Around 60 days is one of the important periods, and it was this same kind of a period that brought the SEC-ONDARY RALLY after the Bull Market ended July 8, 1932. The fact that prices were 5 points below the high of March

10 was an indication of weakness. The main Trend soon turned down.

1937, October 19, low 115.50, down 80 points from the high of March 10, and down 75 points from the high of August 14, and down to below the Old Bottom of 1919, but not 5 points below it. Time for a quick, corrective rally on an oversold condition.

October 29, high 141.50, up 26 points in 10 days' time. The advance died out quickly, and the three-day chart soon showed that the main Trend would continue down.

Final Liquidation in the Bear Market

Always watch the last decline or the last advance which shows the final end of the campaign.

1938, March 15, high 127.50.

March 31, low 97.50, down 30 points in 16 days. This was an average of nearly 2 points per calendar day for this decline and was too fast. This decline from March 10, 1937, had run a little over one year's time and the price decline had been 50 per cent of the highest selling price. A percentage of this kind is always important for a Change in Trend.

1938, July 25, high 146.50. Time from May 27, 65 days, with the price up 40 points, time for a corrective reaction.

1938, September 28, low 127.50, down 19 points in 19 days. This was a normal reaction and following our rules that declines and advances often run around 20 points in a normal market, this would be time to buy again for a further advance in the Bull Market.

End of Short Bull Market

1938, November 10, high 158.75. Time from March 31, 224 days, an advance of 61¼ points and time for a sharp, quick decline.

November 28, low 136, down 22¾ points. Time 18 days. This indicated by breaking back more than 20 points that the Bull Market was over and that a further decline would follow.

Sharp Decline and Clean Out

1939, March 27, high 143.50.

1939, April 11, low 120, a decline of 23½ points in 15 days. This was a clean out of an overbought position and laid the foundation for a better rally.

From November 10, 1938, to April 11, 1939, time 152 days, down 38¾ points, a normal decline for the prices at which the Averages were selling.

War Move

1939, September 1, low 127½. On this date Hitler invaded Poland, and the war started. People bought stocks right and left and shorts started to cover. People believed that we would have the same kind of a Bull Market we had during the war from 1914 to 1918.

September 13, high 157.75, up 30 points in 12 days. This advance was too rapid, and due to the fact that prices failed to cross the top of November 10, 1938, at 158.75, it was an indication that there was heavy selling around these old Levels, while the market held a narrow trading range for some time giving every indication that it had reached Final Top and was getting ready to go lower.

1940, May 8, high 149. From this level a sharp, severe decline occurred. May 21, low 110.50, down 38½ points in 13 days. The Averages made triple Bottoms around this level on May 21, May 28, and June 10, giving an indication of good support and indicating that this was a sharp drive when Hitler was invading France and making great success.

A rally followed to November 8, 1940, which was two years from the high in 1938.

November 8, 1940, high 138.50. After this rally the market continued to make lower Tops and lower Bottoms until the final Bottom came.

1942, April 28, low 92.69. From March 31, 1938, the time was 49 months. The low on March 31, 1938, was 97.50. The low on March 18, 1935, was 96. Therefore, at this time the Averages failed to go five points under the Old Bottom and made this a buying level which was confirmed in a short period of time by the three-day chart.

From the low of April 28, 1942, reactions in price and time were very short showing Up Trend and no 10-point reaction occurred until 1943.

1943, July 15, high 146.50, up in the old selling zone and under a series of bottoms. A reaction was overdue.

August 2, low 133.50, down 13 points in 18 days. This was a natural corrective reaction. The advance from 92.69 to 146.50 was up 53.81 points.

1943, November 30, low 128.50, down 18 points from July 15 high. Time 138 days. This was a normal reaction in a Bull Market, and the main Trend continued up.

1945, March 6, high 162.50. This price had crossed the high of 158.75 made November 10, 1938, and indicated that it was still a Bull Market and prices were going higher, but a sharp, corrective reaction was in order.

1945, March 26, low 151.50, down 11 points in 20 days. Note that the high on April 8, 1940, was 152, from which a big decline followed. Therefore, when prices declined on March 26, 1945, to 151.50 they were down to this old top level and a buying or support level.

1945, May 8, the German War came to an end. This was bullish on stocks, and the market started to advance.

1945, May 31, high 169.50. This was in a new high level for the present move.

July 27, low 159.95, down 9.55 points in 57 days. Failing to react 10 points was an indication of a Bull Market as this is one of our normal reaction points. Prices held above the highs of November 10, 1938, which showed strong up trend.

1945, August 14, the Japanese War came to an end. This was bullish, and an advance followed.

1945, November 8, high 192.75. This was up under Old Selling Levels, Old Bottoms and Old Tops, and a natural reaction was in order.

November 14, low 182.75, down 10 points in 6 days, the same reaction as occurred previously, and a normal reaction indicating that the main Trend was still up.

1945, December 10, high 196.50, up to the Old Tops and Bottoms and Levels where a reaction could occur.

December 20, low 187.50, down 9 points in 10 days, and a normal reaction. Note that the prices had crossed the 1937 high which indicated higher prices, especially as over 7 years' time had elapsed.

1946, February 4, high 207.49. The market at this time was advancing on the largest volume for many months indicating that a sharp, corrective reaction was due.

February 26, low 184.05, a decline of 23.44 points in 22 days. This was the sharpest reaction that had occurred since April 28, 1942, and was the First Warning that the Bull Market was nearing the end.

An advance followed to April 10, high 208.93, which was above the high of February 4 and an indication that prices were going higher. However, this was a temporary Double Top and a reaction followed.

May 6, low 199.26, a decline of 9.67 points in 26 days, a normal reaction and the fact that prices held above the 200 level indicated good support and a further advance to follow.

Final Top—End of Bull Market

1946, May 29, high 213.36. This was the end of the Bull Market which began April 28, 1942. It had lasted exactly 49 months, the same Time Period between the bottom in 1938 and the bottom in 1942. The price was up $120\frac{3}{4}$ points. The fact that prices advanced only about 6 points over the February 4 high was an indication that the first SIGNAL of the break in February was correct in warning that the Bull Market was coming to an end. The three-day chart after May 29 high soon confirmed that the main Trend had turned down.

June 21, low 198.50, down 13¾ points in 23 days. This was the FIRST SIGNAL that the Bull Market had ended, but a SECONDARY RALLY was in order.

July 1, high 208.50, up around the same level as the high in February, up 10 points in 10 days, a normal reaction in the Bear Market.

1946, July 24, low 195.50, down at the old 1937 tops and the top of December, 1945. A support level for a rally.

August 14, 1946, last high 205¼. A big decline followed, and the Averages broke 184, the low of February 26, showing the main Trend was down. Note also August 14, 1937, was the last high of the SECONDARY RALLY after the main Trend had turned down.

The Bull Market from April, 1942, to May, 1949, was one of the longest in time periods except 1929. Therefore, a sharp, corrective reaction in a short period of time was in order.

1946, October 30, low 160.49, down 53 points from May 29 high, time 154 days. Note that the last low on July 27, 1945, was 159.95 making this a support level and buying point. The decline from May high to October low was 25% of the highest selling price 213.36 and occurring in 154 days, was a correction of an overbought market which had only had normal reactions up to that time.

From the low of October 30, 1946, a rally followed.

1947, February 10, high 184.50, up 24 points in 103 days, and under the bottoms of February, 1946, a period of one year's time, making this important for a Change in Trend as February 5th to 10th always is important for a change.

Secondary Decline

1947, May 5, high 175.50, May 19, low 161.50, 14 points down in 14 days. This is all according to our rule that normal markets decline about one point per calendar day. The fact that this bottom was higher than October 30, 1946, made it a Double Bottom and a buying level, which was confirmed by the three-day chart.

1947, July 25, high 187.50, up 26 points in 67 days. This is one of our normal rally periods running from 60 to 72 days, and a reaction was in order.

1947, September 9, and September 26, lows 174.50, down 13 points in 46 days. A rally followed.

October 20, high 176.50, up 12 points in 24 days and a lower top than July indicated good selling and the Trend continued down.

1948, February 11, low 164.04, down 23.40 points from July, 1947. This was a higher bottom than October, 1946, and May, 1947, indicating good support and a buying level. Prices held in a narrow trading range for one month and then the Trend turned up, based on the three-day chart.

1948, June 14, high 194.49, up 34 points from February 11, time 126 days and no reaction lasted over 6 days, and no reaction over 4 points, making this an overbought market when a natural reaction was in order. The fact that the price was up to the Old Bottoms and Tops, 1937 highs and 1929 lows, made this a resistance and selling level.

1948, July 12, last high 192.50; July 19, low 179.50, down 13 points in 7 days, and a signal for lower prices.

September 27, low 175.50, down to an old support level indicating a rally as September is always important for a change in Trend.

October 26, high 190.50, up 15 points in 29 days, and a lower top. This was the same price at which stocks turned down on August 14, 1937. It is always important to keep in mind the Time Periods and these old prices. At this time the prices were lower than they were in June and July, 1948, and it was two years from October, 1946, which was important for a change in Trend.

After Election, Sharp, Quick Declines

November 1, high 190; November 30, low 170.50; down 18 points in 29 days, down to a support level for a rally.

1949, January 7 and 24th, high 182.50, up 11 points, time 38 days. Rule 8 says that when prices reach high between January 7 and 24 and then break the low made in the early part of January, the Trend will turn down. The fact that after January 24 prices could not cross the high of January 7, indicated the Top and it was time to sell.

February 25, low 170½ and only one point lower than the low of November 30, 1948, a support level for a rally.

March 30, 179.15, up 8.65 points from February 25 low, up less than 9 points in 33 days. The fact that the market could not advance 9 points was an indication of weakness and lower prices could be expected.

Remember Rule 8 which says that important changes occur around May 5 to 10. May 5 last high, 177.25, which was lower than the high on March 30, and lower than the high on April 18 indicating that the main Trend was still down. The decline continued.

1949, June 14, low 160.62, time from March 30, 76 days, down 18.43 points. This was the third time around this same low level.

1946, October 30, low 160.49. 1947, May 19, low 161.38. 1948, November 30, low 170.50. The last decline from May 5 to June 14 was a decline of 16.63 points in a period of exactly 40 days, and the fact that prices were at these low levels for the third time and exactly one year from June 14, 1948, high indicated a buying point and time for a rally.

The advance followed June 14 Low and up to this writing, July 17, 1949, the Averages have advanced to above 175, the greatest advance to date from any low during 1949.

CHAPTER VI

TIME PERIODS FOR IMPORTANT SWINGS ON THE AVERAGES

When you have a record of the time required for each important swing of the industrial averages and you know the amount of the advance or decline, you are able to tell something about how long a time period the market will run in the future and you can watch for a change in trend at the end of the important time cycle which has repeated the greatest number of times in the past.

Following the price the letter "A" means advance and the number of days follow. Where the letter "D" follows the price, the days following mean the days the market has declined from the last level.

1912	Oct.	8...high	94.25		
1913	June	11 ....low	72.11 D	246 days	
	Sept.	13......	83.50 A	94 days	
	Dec.	15......	75.25 D	95 days	
1914	Mar.	20......	83.50 A	95 days	
	Dec.	24......	53.17 D	279 days	
1915	Apr.	30......	71.78 A	127 days	
	May	14......	60½ D	14 days	
	Dec.	27......	99½ A	199 days	
1916	July	13......	86½ D	198 days	
	Nov.	21......110½	}A 30 days		
	Dec.	21...... 90½	}		
1917	Jan.	2......	99¼ A	14 days	
	Feb.	2......	87 D	31 days	
	June	9......	99¼ A	127 days	
	Dec.	19......	65.90 D	192 days	
1918	Oct.	18......	89.50 A	304 days	
1919	Feb.	8......	79.15 D	103 days	
	July	14......112.50 A	156 days		
	Aug.	20......	98.50 D	37 days	
	Nov.	3......119.62	}A 26 days		
	Nov.	29......103.50	}		
1920	Jan.	3......109.50 A	35 days		
	Feb.	25......	89.50 D	53 days	
	Apr.	8......105.50 A	42 days		
	May	19......	87.50 D	41 days	
	July	8......	94.50 A	50 days	
	Aug.	10......	83.50 D	33 days	
	Sept.	17......	89.75 A	38 days	
	Dec.	21......	65.90 D	96 days	
1921	May	5......	80.05 A	135 days	
	June	20......	64.75 D	46 days	
	July	6......	69.75 A	16 days	

	Aug.	24........	63.90 D	49 days	
1922	Oct.	14........103.50 A	52 days		
	Nov.	14........	93.50 D	31 days	
1924	Feb.	6........101.50 A	84 days		
	May	14......	88.75 D	98 days	
	May	20......105.50 A	98 days		
	Oct.	14........	99.50 D	55 days	
1925	Jan.	22........123.50 A	100 days		
	Feb.	16........117.50 D	25 days		
	Mar.	6........125.50 A	18 days		
	Mar.	30........115.00 D	24 days		
	Apr.	18........122½ A	19 days		
	Apr.	27..... .119.60 D	9 days		
	Nov.	6........159.25 A	192 days		
	Nov.	24........148.50 D	18 days		
1926	Feb.	11........162.50 A	78 days		
	Mar.	3........144.50 D	20 days		
	Mar.	12........153.50 A	9 days		
	Mar.	30........135.50 D	18 days		
	Apr.	24........144.50 A	25 days		
	May	19........137.25 D	25 days		
	Aug.	24........162.50 A	97 days		
	Oct.	19........145.50 D	56 days		
	Dec.	18..,.....161.50 A	60 days		
1927	Jan.	25........152.50 D	38 days		
	May	28........172.50 A	123 days		
	June	27........165.50 D	30 days		
	Oct.	3........195.50 A	97 days		
	Oct.	22........179.50 D	19 days		
1928	Jan.	3........203.50 A	73 days		
	Jan.	18........191.50 D	15 days		
	Mar.	20........214.50 A	62 days		
	Apr.	23........207.00 D	34 days		

May 14.......220.50 A 21 days
May 22.......211.50 D 8 days
1928 June 2.......220.50 D 13 days
June 18.......202.00 D 16 days
July 5.......214.50 A 19 days
July 16.......205.00 D 11 days
Oct. 24.......260.50 A 100 days
Oct. 31.......249 D 7 days
Nov. 28.......298.50 A 28 days
Dec. 10.......254.36 D 12 days
1929 Feb. 1.......325 A 53 days
Feb. 18.......293 D 17 days
Mar. 1.......325 A 13 days
Mar. 26.......281.50 D 25 days
May 6..:.......331 A 41 days
May 31.......291 D 24 days
July 8.......350.50 A 38 days
July 29.......337 D 21 days
Sept. 3.......386.10 A 36 days
Oct. 4.......321 D 31 days
Oct. 11.......358.50 A 7 days
Oct. 29.......210.50 D 18 days
Nov. 8.......245 A 10 days
Nov. 13.......195.50 D 5 days
Dec. 9.......267 A 27 days
Dec. 20.......227 D 11 days
1930 Feb. 5.......274 A 47 days
Feb. 25.......259.50 D 20 days
Apr. 16.......297.75 A 50 days
May 5.......249 D 19 days
June 2.......275 A 28 days
June 25.......207.50 D 23 days
July 28.......243.50 A 33 days
Aug. 9.......234.50 D 12 days
Sept. 10.......247 A 32 days
Oct. 18.......183.50 D 38 days
Oct. 28.......298.50 A 10 days
Nov. 10.......168.25 D 13 days
Nov. 25.......191.50 A 15 days
Dec. 17.......154.50 D 22 days
1931 Feb. 24...196.75 A 59 days
Apr. 29...142 D 64 days
May 9...156.00 A 10 days
June 2...119.50 D 24 days
June 27...157.50 A 25 days
Aug. 6...132.50 D 40 days
Aug. 15...146.50 A 9 days
Oct. 5...85.50 D 51 days
Nov. 9...119.50 A 35 days
1932 Jan. 5...69.50 D 57 days
Jan. 14...87.50 A 9 days
Feb. 10...70 D 27 days
Feb. 19...89.50 A 9 days
June 2...43.50 D 103 days
June 16...51.50 A 14 days
1932 July 8...40.60 D 22 days
Sept. 8...81.50 A 62 days
Oct. 10...57.50 D 32 days
Nov. 12...68.50 A 33 days

Dec. 3.........55.50 D 21 days
1933 Jan. 11.........65.25 A 39 days
Feb. 27.........49.50 D 47 days
July 18.........110.50 A 141 days
July 21.........84.50 D 3 days
Sept. 18.........107.50 A 59 days
Oct. 21.........82.20 D 33 days
1934 Feb. 5.........111.50 A 107 days
Mar. 27.........97.50 D 50 days
Apr. 20.........107 A 24 days
May 14.........89.50 D 24 days
June 19.........101.25 A 36 days
July 26.........84.50 D 37 days
Aug. 25.........96.25 A 30 days
Sept. 17.........85.75 D 23 days
1935 Jan. 7.........106.50 A 112 days
Feb. 6.........99.75 D 30 days
Feb. 18.........108.50 A 12 days
Mar. 18.........96 D 28 days
Sept. 11.........135.50 A 177 days
Oct. 3.........126.50 D 22 days
Nov. 20.........149.50 A 48 days
Dec. 16.........138.50 D 26 days
1936 Apr. 6.........163.25 A 112 days
Apr. 24.........141.50 D 18 days
Aug. 10.........170.50 A 108 days
Aug. 21.........160.50 D 11 days
Nov. 18.........186.25 A 89 days
Dec. 21.........175.25 D 33 days
1937 Mar. 10.........195.50 A 79 days
Apr. 9.........175.50 D 30 days
Apr. 22.........184.50 A 13 days
June 14.........163.75 D 53 days
Aug. 14.........190.50 A 61 days
Oct. 19.........115.50 D 67 days
Oct. 29.........140.50 A 10 days
Nov. 23.........112.50 D 25 days
Dec. 8.........131.25 A 15 days
Dec. 29.........117.50 D 21 days
1938 Jan. 15.........134.50 A 17 days
Feb. 4.........117.25 D 20 days
Feb. 23.........133 A 19 days
Mar. 31.........97.50 D 36 days
1938 Apr. 18.........121.50 A 18 days
May 27.........106.50 D 39 days
July 25.........146.50 A 59 days
Aug. 12.........135.50 D 18 days
Aug. 24.........145.50 A 12 days
Sept. 28.........127.50 D 35 days
Nov. 10.........158.75 A 43 days
Nov. 28.........145.50 D 18 days
1939 Jan. 5.........155.50 A 38 days
Jan. 26.........136.25 D 21 days
Mar. 10.........152.50 A 43 days
Apr. 11.........120.25 D 31 days
June 2.........140.50 A 52 days
June 30.........128.75 D 28 days
July 25.........145.50 A 25 days
Aug. 24.........128.50 D 30 days

	Aug.	30........138.25 A	6 days
	Sept.	1.......127.50 D	2 days
	Sept.	13........157½ A	12 days
	Sept.	18.....147½ D	5 days
	Oct.	26........156 A	38 days
	Nov.	30........144.50 D	35 days
1940	Jan.	3........153.50 A	34 days
	Jan.	15........143.50 D	12 days
	Mar.	28.......152 A	73 days
	May	21.......110.61 D	54 days
	May	23........117.50 A	2 days
	May	28........110.50 D	5 days
	June	3.......116.50 A	6 days
	June	10.......110.50 D	7 days
	July	31........127.50 A	51 days
	Aug.	16........120.50 D	16 days
	Sept.	5........134.50 A	20 days
	Sept.	13........127.50 D	8 days
	Sept.	24........135.50 A	11 days
	Oct.	15........129.50 D	19 days
	Nov.	8.......138.50 A	24 days
	Dec.	23.......127.50 D	45 days
1941	Jan.	10........134.50 A	18 days
	Feb.	19........117.25 D	40 days
	Apr.	4.......125.50 A	44 days
	May	1.......114.50 D	27 days
	July	22........131.50 A	82 days
	Aug.	15........124.50 D	24 days
	Sept.	18........130 25 A	34 days
	Dec.	24.......105.50 D	97 days
1942	Jan.	6........114.50 A	13 days
	Apr.	28....... 92.69 D	112 days
	June	9.......106.50 A	42 days
	June	25.......102 D	17 days
1942	July	9........109.50 A	14 days
	Aug.	7........104.40 D	29 days
	Nov.	9........118.50 A	94 days
	Nov.	25........113.50 D	16 days
1943	Apr.	6.......137.50 A	132 days
	Apr.	13.......129.75 D	7 days
	July	15.......146.50 A	93 days
	Aug.	2........133.50 D	18 days
	Sept.	20.......142.50 A	49 days
	Nov.	30.......128.50 D	71 days
1944	Jan.	11........138.50 A	42 days
	Feb.	7........134.25 D	27 days
	Mar.	16.......141.50 A	38 days
	Apr.	25.......134.75 D	40 days
	July	10.......150.50 A	76 days
	Sept.	7.......142.50 D	59 days
	Oct.	6........149.50 A	29 days
	Oct.	27........145.50 D	21 days
	Dec.	16.........153 A	50 days
	Dec.	27.......147.75 D	11 days

1945	Mar.	6.......162.25 A	69 days
	Mar.	26.......151.50 D	20 days
	May	31.......169.50 A	66 days
	July	27........159.95 D	57 days
	Nov.	8.......192.75 A	104 days
	Nov.	14........182.75 D	6 days
	Dec.	10.......196.50 A	26 days
	Dec.	20.......187.50 D	10 days
1946	Feb.	4........207.50 A	46 days
	Feb.	26.......184.04 D	22 days
	Apr.	18.......209.50 A	51 days
	May	6.......199.50 D	18 days
	May	29.......213.36 A	23 days
	June	12.......207.50 D	14 days
	June	17.......211.50 A	5 days
	June	21.......198.50 D	4 days
	July	1.......208.50 A	10 days
	July	24.......194.50 D	23 days
	Aug.	14.......205.25 A	21 days
	Sept.	19.......164.50 D	36 days
	Sept.	26.......176.50 A	7 days
	Oct.	10.......161.50 D	14 days
	Oct.	16.......177.25 A	6 days
	Oct.	30.......160.62 D	14 days
	Nov.	6.......175 A	7 days
	Nov.	22.......162.50 D	16 days
1947	Jan.	7.......179.50 A	46 days
	Jan.	16.......170.25 D	9 days
	Feb.	10.......184.50 A	25 days
	Feb.	15........172 D	5 days
	Mar.	28.......179.50 A	41 days
	Apr.	15.......165.50 D	18 days
1947	May	5.......175.50 A	20 days
	May	19.......161.50 D	14 days
	July	14.......187.50 A	56 days
	Sept.	9.......174.50 D	57 days
	Oct.	20.......186 A	41 days
	Dec.	6.......175.50 D	47 days
1948	Jan.	5.......181.50 A	30 days
	Feb.	11........164.04 D	37 days
	June	14.......194.49 A	124 days
	July	19.......179.50 D	35 days
	July	28.......187 A	9 days
	Aug.	11.......176.50 D	14 days
	Sept.	7.......185.50 A	27 days
	Sept.	27.......175.50 D	20 days
	Oct.	26.......190.50 A	29 days
	Nov.	30.......171.50 D	35 days
1949	Jan.	7.......182.50 A	38 days
	Jan.	17.......177.50 D	10 days
	Jan.	24.......182.50 A	7 days
	Feb.	25.......170.50 D	32 days
	Mar.	30.......179.15 A	33 days
	Apr.	22.......172.50 D	23 days
	May	5.......177.25 A	13 days
	June	14.......160.69 D	40 days

CHAPTER VII

DOW JONES 30 INDUSTRIAL AVERAGES 3-DAY CHART MOVES

My reason for using the Dow-Jones 30 Industrial Averages as a trend indicator is not because the Dow theory is working perfectly, but that these industrial Averages do indicate the trend of most of the individual stocks. However, the time period on some individual stocks will run out sooner than the Averages on the up side and some will run later. The same in the Bear Market. Some stocks will make low sooner by several months, and some later than the Averages. But the Averages are a good guide to the dates when final highs and lows will be reached, and they are important in getting resistance levels for buying and selling prices. The railroads are slowly becoming obsolete and do not work in harmony with the industrial Averages any more. The public utility averages are in strong position and work more in harmony with the industrial Averages than the rails do. My advice is to keep up the Dow-Jones 30 Industrial Averages and follow the trend of these stocks and then watch individual stocks that conform to the same trend, and trade in them. The percentage between the railroad averages and the 30 Industrial Averages has not been maintained the same during the past few years because industrial stocks in most cases on advances are stronger and advance faster than the rails. Therefore, it is folly to try to watch the rails to confirm with the industrials as based on the Dow theory. But the thing to do is to watch individual stocks that show strong or weak positions and trade in them and use the Industrial Averages as a trend indicator applying all the rules which I have given.

These Averages are not a true average. From 1897 to 1914 they are figured on a basis of 12 stocks. Then in December, 1914, they were changed to 20 stocks and later changed to 30 stocks. Although the Averages work all right and do give a definite indication of the trend, they do not represent the actual value of stocks as they sell today, because these Averages as they are figured have the dividends and split-ups figured in the averages. What I call a true average is the cost of buying 100 shares of the 30 stocks at any time, leaving out all dividends and split-ups. For example, June 14, 1949, the Dow-Jones Averages showed a low of 160.69 based on the present way of figuring. But by taking the 30 stocks and using the extreme low that day, dividing by 30, we get an average of 52.27, which is the correct average and what it would cost to buy these stocks at that time.

After June 14 DuPont was split up and the price changed.

June 28, 1949, figuring the Averages on the low of that day after the split up of DuPont, the Averages were 48.59, against the regular way of figuring the averages showing a low of 164.65.

While the average figure on the basis of the Dow-Jones formula for figuring was 164.65, there was only one stock in the entire list that was selling higher than this level, which was Allied Chemical selling at 167. American Telephone was 139. The next highest price, American Can, was 89.25 and National Steel at 75. All of the other stocks were selling at much lower levels, some of them selling as low as $17.00 and $18.00 per share and several of them around 20. This way of figuring the averages, of course, distorts the picture and makes the price look much higher than it actually is based on the day's prices. However, you can go ahead and use the Dow-Jones Thirty Industrial Averages and get the trend just the same as you could if they were figured on the basis of actual selling price.

Three-Day Moves or More

These figures are to be used with the 3 day chart. They are recorded in 3-day moves or more, except when extreme highs or lows are reached and we wish to catch a turn when the market is very active; in this case we sometimes use 1 and 2-day moves. All of these moves are based on calendar days. The rules to use is, when any 3-day Bottom is broken, it

indicates lower prices and when the top, or high levels, of a
3-day level is crossed, it is an indication of higher prices.
However, all other rules must be applied and you must always consider the last low, or starting point, from which the
market moves up and the last high from which the decline
starts, as these major swings are of greater importance. An
advancing market continues to make higher bottoms on the
main swings. A declining market continues to make lower
tops on the main swings, but there are times when the market
will remain in a narrow Trading Range without breaking the
low of a previous swing and not crossing the high of a previous top. Until the averages or an individual stock breaks
out of the trading range, you must not consider that the main
trend has changed.

The Time Period is most important. The longer the time
which has elapsed when a Top is crossed, or a Bottom is
broken, the greater the advance or decline should be.

Always consider the fact of how long a market has been
advancing from the extreme low level, or how long it has
been declining from an extreme high level. Often at the end
of any campaign, prices may move up into new high levels,
or decline to slightly lower levels and then not continue on,
because the time cycle is running out.

Examples: March 31, 1938, the Dow-Jones 30 Industrial
Averages declined to 97½. The last Bottom around this
same price level was March 18, 1935, when the Averages
sold at 96.

1942, April 28, the Dow-Jones Averages declined to
92.62. This was not quite 5 points below the 1938 lows and
was less than 4 points under the 1935 low. Our rules say
that prices can decline 5 points below an old Bottom, or advance 5 points above an old Top without changing the main
trend.

In April, 1942, stocks had been declining from the extreme high of March 10, 1937, and were down over 5 years,
running out a long time cycle. Therefore, when prices broke
these old levels, and failed to go 5 points lower, you would
buy stocks, figuring that the trend was getting ready to

change. Note the moves on the 3-day chart, 1942, April 21, last high 98.02 and April 28, extreme low, 92.69. This was a 7-day decline and less than 6 points decline.

May 11, 1942, the Averages advanced to 99.49; this was above the last top of April 21 on the 3-Day Chart and indicated higher prices. From May 11th, a 3-day decline occurred, making a low of 96.39, or down 3.30 points. The price never sold lower than this level until May 29, 1946, when final high was reached. By studying the 3-Day Chart and the progressive, or higher Bottoms and higher Tops, you will see how this chart continued to indicate higher prices with nothing but normal reactions, both in time periods and in price reactions.

30 Industrial Averages 3-Day Chart Moves

The figures published in this book show all of the 3-day moves on the Averages from 1912 to July 19, 1949. The 3-Day Chart in the back of the book starts November 8, 1940, and shows every 3-day move during that period.

Rule for Keeping Up 3-Day Chart

When a market is advancing and starts up from a low point and makes higher Bottoms and higher Tops for 3 consecutive days, the Chart is moved up to the top of the third day. Should the market then react for 2 days, you would not record this movement on the chart, but when it moved up above the First Top, continue to move the line up to the top of each day until there were 3 days lower Bottoms. Then you would move the line down to the low of the third day and continue to follow it down as long as prices went lower. If 2-day rallies occurred, you would ignore them, except when the market is near extreme high or extreme low prices. In cases of this kind you would record the 2-day moves, especially if the fluctuations were very wide. After a market has been advancing for a considerable time and makes a Double or Triple Top and breaks the last low on the 3-Day Chart, you consider that the minor trends, at least, have turned down. When a market is declining and crosses the last Top on the 3-Day Chart, you would consider that the trend had turned up at least temporarily. You will find it helpful to apply all of the other rules given with the 3-Day Chart indication.

Examples of Three-Day Moves.

Starting from November 8, 1940, high 138.50, the trend turned down on the 3-Day Chart and continued to make lower Tops and lower Bottoms.

1941, April 23, May 1, 16 and 26, lows were reached. On May 26 the second higher Bottom was recorded. This was the time to buy with a Stop Loss Order under the low of May 1. When prices crossed the high of May 21, the trend showed up. July 22 high, $131\frac{1}{2}$. The Averages broke under the 3-Day Bottoms, and on August 15 made a low of $124\frac{1}{2}$. The market rallied to September 18, reaching high at $130\frac{1}{4}$, a lower Top than July 22 and a Selling Level. The trend continued down, and the lows of August 15 were broken indicating that the main trend was down. The decline continued with only one 3-Day Top being crossed on January 6, 1942. This was only 2 points above the high of December 16, 1941, and January 6 is around one of the dates that we always expect the trends to change. The trend continued down to April 28, 1942, extreme low, 92.69, down 38.31 points from July 22, 1941, and the 3-Day Chart would have kept you short all the time.

From April 28 lows, the Averages started making higher Bottoms and higher Tops. It was the time to buy anyway against the old Bottoms of 1935 and 1938.

June, 1942, the Averages crossed the high of $102\frac{1}{2}$ made on April 7. This definitely showed up trend. The advance continued making higher Bottoms and higher Tops until July 15, 1943, high $146\frac{1}{2}$. This was a Selling Level as shown by the rules. The 3-Day Chart turned down and prices declined to November 30, making low at 128.94. Note that on March 10 and 22 lows were around $128\frac{1}{2}$, making 129 a Buying Level against Old Bottoms on the 3-Day Chart. The trend turned up after November 30, and each Swing Bottom was higher until February 4, 1946, high $207\frac{1}{2}$, a

Selling Level. A sharp, quick decline followed to February 26, low 184.04. Note last low levels around 183 on October 30 and November 14, 1945, making 184 a Buying Level against Old Bottoms. From February the trend moved on up again to May 29, 1946, FINAL HIGH 213¼. This was a Selling Level on many of our rules. June 12, low 207½ at the top of February 4 and a Rally Point. June 17, high 208½, same level as February 4, a Selling Level. The decline started and the Averages broke the low of June 12, showing main trend down. There was no 3-Day Top crossed until FINAL LOW October 30, 1946, at 160.69, a Buying Level against the low of July 27, 1945, and also based on other rules explained under Time Periods and Percentage Points.

From October 30 low, no lows were broken on the 3-Day Chart by 3 points until February 10, 1947, high 184½. This was under the Old Bottoms of February 26, 1946, and a Selling Level. The main trend turned down again, and each Swing Top was lower until May 19, 1947, low 161½, a Buying Level against the old Bottoms of October 30, 1946. A rapid advance followed. July 14, high 187½, July 18, low 182, July 25, high 187½, a Double Top and Selling Level. The Averages broke the low of July 18 and continued down to September 9 and 26, making low at 174½, the same low as June 25, a Double Bottom and Buying Level.

October 20, high 186½, a lower Top than July 14 and 25 and a Selling Level. The trend turned down, prices making Lower Tops and Lower Bottoms on the 3-Day Chart until February 11, 1948, when low was reached at 164.07. Another Bottom was made on February 20 and March 17, making this a Double Bottom and Buying Level. When prices crossed the Top of March 3, the trend was definitely up, making this a SAFE BUYING LEVEL. The advance was rapid, and no 3-Day Bottom was broken until June 14, 1948, high 194.49 at the 50 per cent point of 386 and at Old Bottom and Top Levels, making this a place to sell out long stocks and go short. The trend turned down.

August 11 and 21 and September 27 lows were made at 176½ to 175½. Double and Triple Bottoms and a Buying Level. A quick rally followed until October 26, high 190.50. There was a reaction to October 29, and a rally to November 1. The lows of October 29 were broken showing down trend, and a fast decline followed after the election.

November 30, low 170½, a Support and Buying Level against Old Bottoms. A rally followed.

1949, January 7, high 182½, and after a reaction there was another rally to January 24, making this a Double Top and Selling Level, and based on our other rules when the Averages could not cross the Tops of January 7 by the 24th, they indicated lower.

February 25, low 170½, a Double Bottom against November 30 lows and a Buying Level. March 30, high 179.15. The fact that the Averages failed to rally 9 points was an indication of weakness based on the 9-Point Chart. The trend turned down after March 30, and Bottoms and Tops were lower on the 3-Day Chart until June 14, low 160.62. This was a Triple Bottom against October 30, 1946, May 19, 1947, and a Buying Point protected with Stop Loss Order. A rally followed to July 19, with the Averages up above 174 and no 3-Day Reaction has occurred. In fact, only 1-day Reactions have taken place. This indicates strength, but there will come a time when the Averages will react 3 days or more. After that when they cross the top of the First Reaction, it will be a definite indication that the main trend has turned up, and prices should go higher.

RECORD OF 3-DAY MOVES ON AVERAGES 1912 TO 1949

(See analysis of 3-Day Moves November 8, 1940 and Chart in Back of Book.)

1912	Sept. 30.... 94.15	1914	Feb.	25.... 81.31	1916	Mar. 25.... 93.23
	Oct. 4.... 93.70			28.... 82.26		Apr. 6.... 94.46
	8.... 94.12		Mar. 6.... 81.12			22.... 84.96

Date	Value
1912 Oct. 14	92.40
16	93.70
Nov. 4	90.29
7	91.67
11	89.58
14	90.40
18	89.97
21	91.40
Dec. 11	85.25
1913 Jan. 9	88.57
14	84.96
18	85.75
20	81.55
30	83.80
Feb. 18	79.82
20	80.20
25	78.72
Mar. 5	81.69
20	78.25
Apr. 4	83.19
19	81.00
22	81.46
29	78.39
May 5	79.95
15	78.51
24	79.88
June 11	72.11
18	75.85
21	74.03
July 28	79.06
Aug. 1	78.21
13	80.93
15	79.50
29	81.81
Sept. 4	80.27
13	83.43
17	82.38
22	83.01
30	80.37
Oct. 2	81.43
16	77.09
21	79.60
23	78.40
27	79.38
Nov. 10	75.94
18	77.25
Dec. 1	75.77
4	77.01
15	75.27
26	78.85
30	78.26
1914 Jan. 26	82.88
29	81.72
Feb. 2	83.19
11	82.50
14	83.09

Date	Value
Mar. 20	83.43
30	81.64
Apr. 2	82.47
25	76.97
May 1	80.11
8	79.16
19	81.66
22	80.85
June 10	81.84
25	79.30
July 8	81.79
30	71.42
Dec. 12	54.72
14	56.76
24	53.17
1915 Jan. 23	58.52
Feb. 1	55.59
11	57.83
24	54.22
Mar. 8	56.98
13	56.35
Apr. 30	71.78
May 10	62.06
12	64.46
14	60.38
22	65.50
26	64.42
June 22	71.90
July 9	67.88
Aug. 18	81.86
21	76.76
28	81.95
Sept. 3	80.70
Oct. 2	91.98
6	88.23
22	96.46
28	93.34
Nov. 4	96.06
9	91.08
16	96.33
20	95.02
29	97.56
Dec. 2	94.78
8	98.45
13	95.96
27	99.21
1916 Jan. 11	94.07
17	96.63
20	93.60
25	94.24
31	90.58
Feb. 11	96.15
17	94.11
19	94.77
Mar. 2	90.52
16	96.08

Date	Value
May 1	90.30
May 4	87.71
15	92.43
17	91.51
25	92.62
June 2	91.22
12	93.61
26	87.68
July 5	90.53
13	86.42
22	89.75
27	88.00
Aug. 1	89.05
8	88.15
22	93.83
Sept. 1	91.19
Nov. 9	107.68
13	105.63
21	110.15
23	107.48
25	109.95
29	105.97
Dec. 6	106.76
21	90.16
1917 Jan. 2	99.18
13	95.13
20	97.97
23	96.26
26	97.36
Feb. 2	87.01
6	92.81
9	90.20
13	92.37
15	91.65
20	94.91
Mar. 1	91.10
20	98.20
Apr. 10	91.20
14	93.76
24	90.66
May 1	93.42
9	89.08
June 9	99.08
20	94.78
25	97.57
July 19	90.48
21	92.61
25	91.24
Aug. 6	93.85
Sept. 4	81.20
10	83.88
17	81.55
25	86.02
Oct. 15	75.13
20	79.80
Nov. 8	68.58

1917 Nov. 12.... 70.65
15.... 69.10
26.... 74.03
Dec. 19.... 65.95
1918 Jan. 2.... 76.68
8.... 74.63
10.... 76.33
15.... 73.38
31.... 79.80
Feb. 7... 77.78
19.... 82.08
25.... 79.17
27.. . 80.50
Mar. 2... 78.98
11.... 79.78
23.... 76.24
Apr. 6.... 77.95
11.... 75.58
20.... 79.73
30.... 77.51
May 15.... 84.04
June 1.... 77.93
26.... 83.02
July 1.... 81.81
6.... 83.20
15.... 80.58
18.... 82.92
23.... 80.51
26.... 81.51
Aug. 1.... 80.71
10... 82.04
17.... 81.51
Sept. 3.... 83.84
13.... 80.29
Oct. 4.... 85.31
9... 83.36
18... 89.07
30.... 84.08
Nov. 9... 88.06
25... 79.87
Dec. 10.... 84.50
26.... 80.44
1919 Jan. 3... 83.35
11.... 81.66
15.... 82.40
21.... 79.88
24.... 81.75
Feb. 8. . 79.15
Mar. 21.. . 89.05
26.... 86.83
Apr. 9.... 91.01
12.... 89.61
May 14....100.37
19.... 99.16
June 5....107.55
16.... 99.56
21....106.45
24....104.58
July 14....112.23

21....107.24
26....111.10
Aug. 7....100.80
12....105.10
20.... 98.46
Sept. 3....108.55
8....106.51
16....108.81
20....104.99
30....111.42
Oct. 3....108.90
Nov. 3....119.62
12....107.15
13....110.69
19....106.15
25....109.02
29....103.60
Dec. 4....107.97
12....103.73
17....107.26
22....103.55
1920 Jan. 3....109.88
16....101.94
20....103.48
23....101.90
30....104.21
Feb. 11... 90.66
21... 95.63
25... 89.98
Mar. 22....104.17
24....100.33
Apr. 8....105.65
23... 95.46
26... 97.20
29... 93.16
May 8... 94.75
19... 87.36
June 12... 93.20
30... 90.76
July 8... 94.51
16... 89.95
22... 90.74
Aug. 10... 83.20
13... 85.89
17... 83.90
24... 87.29
31... 86.16
Sept. 9... 88.33
13... 86.96
17... 89.95
30... 82.95
Oct. 6... 85.60
11... 84.00
25.. 85.73
Oct. 28.... 84.61
Nov. 1... 85.48
19... 73.12
23... 77.20
27.... 75.46

Dec. 4.... 77.63
21... 66.75
1921 Jan. 11.... 76.14
13.... 74.43
19.... 76.76
21.... 74.65
29.... 76.34
Feb. 3... 74.34
16... 77.14
24... 74.66
Mar. 5... 75.25
11.... 72.25
23.... 77.78
Apr. 4... 75.16
6... 76.58
8... 75.61
May 5.. 80.03
June 20... 64.90
July 6... 69.86
15... 67.25
25.... 69.80
Aug. 16... 65.27
24... 63.90
Sept. 10... 71.92
20. 69.43
Oct. 1... 71.68
6... 70.42
11... 71.06
17... 69.46
Nov. 16... 77.13
22... 76.21
Dec. 15... 81.50
22.. 78.76
31... 81.10
1922 Jan. 5.. 78.68
20... 82.95
31... 81.30
Feb. 6.... 83.70
8... 82.74
21... 85.81
27.... 84.58
Mar. 18... 88.47
27... 86.60
Apr. 22... 93.46
27... 91.10
May 3... 93.81
11... 91.50
29... 96.41
June 12... 90.73
20... 93.51
29... 92.06
July 20... 96.76
24... 94.64
Aug. 22....100.75
28... 99.21
Sept. 11....102.05
21... 98.37
23... 99.10
30.... 96.30

1922 Oct. 14....103.43
         31.... 96.11
     Nov. 8.... 99.53
          14.... 93.61
          20.... 95.82
          27.... 92.03
1923 Jan. 3.... 99.42
           9.... 97.23
          13.... 99.09
          16.... 96.96
     Feb. 21....103.59
          26....102.40
     Mar. 7....105.23
          10....103.82
          20....105.38
     Apr. 4....101.40
           7....102.56
          11....101.08
          19....102.58
          23....100.73
          26....101.37
     May   7.... 95.41
           9.... 98.19
          21.... 92.77
          29.... 97.66
     June 1.... 95.36
           6.... 97.24
          20.... 90.81
          23.... 93.30
          30.... 87.85
     July 7.... 89.41
          12.... 87.64
          20.... 91.72
          31.... 86.91
     Aug. 18.... 92.32
          25.... 91.59
          29.... 93.70
     Sept. 4.... 92.25
          11.... 93.61
          25.... 87.94
     Oct. 3.... 90.45
          16.... 86.91
          20.... 87.83
          27.... 85.76
     Nov. 10.... 91.39
          17.... 89.65
          26.... 92.88
          30.... 92.34
     Dec. 17.... 95.26
          22....93.63
1924 Jan. 11.... 97.46
          14.... 95.68
     Feb. 6....101.31
          18.... 96.33
     Mar. 14.... 98.86
          29.... 92.28
     Apr. 4.... 94.69
          14.... 89.91
          17.... 91.34

          21.... 89.18
     May   7.... 92.47
          14.... 88.77
          24.... 90.66
          29.... 89.90
     June 3.... 91.23
           7.... 89.52
          16.... 93.80
          23.... 92.65
     July 12.... 97.60
          17.... 96.85
     Aug. 4....103.28
          12....101.58
          20....105.57
          28....102.67
          30....105.16
     Sept. 6....100.76
          24....104.68
          29....102.96
     Oct. 1....104.08
          14.... 99.18
     Nov. 18....110.73
          22....109.55
1925 Jan. 13....123.56
          16....121.71
          22....123.60
          26....121.90
          31....123.22
     Feb. 3....120.08
           9....122.37
          16....117.96
     Mar. 6....125.68
          10....122.62
          12....124.60
          18....118.25
          20....120.91
          30....115.00
     Apr. 18....122.02
          27....119.46
     May   7....125.16
          13....124.21
     June 2....130.42
          10....126.75
          17....129.80
          23....127.17
     July 8....133.07
          11....131.43
          27....136.50
          31....133.81
     Aug. 25....143.18
     Sept. 2....137.22
          19....147.73
          30....143.46
     Nov. 6....159.39
          10....151.60
          13....157.76
          24....148.18
     Dec. 5....154.63
           9....152.57

          14....154.70
          21....152.35
          24....157.01
          30....155.81
1926 Jan. 9....159.10
          19....153.81
     Feb. 4....160.53
           8....159.10
          11....162.31
          15....158.30
          18....161.09
     Mar. 3....144.44
          10....153.13
          30....135.20
     Apr. 6....142.43
          16....136.27
          24....144.83
     May   3....140.53
           6....142.13
          19....137.16
     June 21....154.03
          26....150.68
     July 17....158.81
          24....154.59
     Aug. 14....166.64
          25....160.41
     Sept. 7....166.10
          20....156.26
          25....159.27
          29....157.71
     Oct. 1....159.69
          11....149.35
          14....152.10
          19....145.66
          27....151.87
          30....150.38
     Nov. 16....156.53
          19....152.86
     Dec. 18....161.86
1927 Jan. 3....155.16
          10....156.56
          17....153.91
          21....155.51
          25....152.73
     Feb. 1....156.26
           7....154.31
          28....161.96
     Mar. 7....158.62
          17....161.78
          22....158.41
     Apr. 22....167.36
          28....163.53
     May 21....172.06
          24....171.06
          28....172.56
     June 3....169.65
           6....171.13
          14....167.63
          16....170.15

1927 June 27....165.73
Aug. 2....185.55
12....177.13
Sept. 7...197.75
12...194.00
15...198.97
28...194.11
Oct. 3....199.78
10....189.03
13....190.45
22....179.78
25....185.31
29....180.32
Nov. 23...197.10
28...194.80
Dec. 3...197.34
8...193.58
20...200.93
28...198.60
1928 Jan. 3....203.35
10....197.52
13...199.51
18...194.50
24...201.01
Feb. 3....196.30
9...199.35
20...191.33
Mar. 30...214.45
Apr. 10...209.23
13...216.93
23...207.94
May 14...220.88
22...211.73
June 2...220.96
12...202.65
14...210.76
18...201.96
July 5...214.43
11...206.43
14...207.77
16...205.10
Aug. 7...218.06
14...214.08
31...240.41
Sept. 10...238.82
12...241.48
27...236.86
Oct. 1...242.46
3...233.60
5...243.08
9...236.79
19...259.19
22...250.08
24...260.39
31...248.76
Nov. 28...299.35
Dec. 3...283.89
4...295.61
10...254.36

31...301.61
1929 Jan. 3...311.46
8...292.89
25...319.36
30...308.47
Feb. 1...324.16
8...298.03
13...316.06
18...293.40
Mar. 1...324.40
6...302.93
15...322.75
26...281.51
Apr. 5...307.97
10...295.71
23...320.10
26...311.00
May 6...331.01
13...313.56
17...325.64
31...290.02
June 8...312.00
11...301.22
July 8...350.09
11...340.12
12...350.26
16...339.98
19...349.19
22...339.32
24...350.30
29...336.36
Aug. 5...358.66
9...336.13
Sept. 3...386.10
13...359.70
19...375.20
Oct. 4...320.45
11...358.77
21...314.55
23...329.94
24...272.32
Oct. 25...306.02
29...212.33
31...281.54
Nov. 7...217.84
8...245.28
13...195.35
22...250.75
27...233.59
Dec. 9...267.56
13...239.58
14...254.41
20...227.20
27...246.35
30...235.95
1930 Jan. 2...252.29
7...243.80
16...253.49
18...243.37

Feb. 5....274.01
10....266.37
13....275.00
25....259.78
Mar. 10...279.40
17....268.94
Apr. 11....296.35
15....189.34
16...297.25
29...272.24
30...283.51
May 5...249.82
14...277.22
20...260.76
June 2...276.86
12...241.00
13...251.63
18...212.27
20...232.69
25...207.74
July 1...229.53
8...214.64
18...242.01
21...228.71
28...243.65
31...229.09
Aug. 5...240.95
9...218.82
Sept. 2...242.77
4...234.35
10...247.21
30...201.95
Oct. 3...216.89
10...186.70
15...201.64
18...183.65
21...193.95
22...181.53
28...198.59
Nov. 10...168.32
15...187.59
18...177.63
25...191.28
28...178.88
Dec. 2...187.96
17...154.45
20...170.91
29...158.41
1931 Jan. 8...175.62
19...160.09
23...172.97
29...164.81
Feb. 11...185.89
14...178.20
24...196.96
Mar. 6...178.46
10...188.10
13...175.89
20...189.31

1931 Apr.	2	168.30
	6	174.69
	17	158.50
	20	164.42
	29	141.78
May	1	153.82
	6	145.65
	9	156.17
June	2	119.89
	27	157.93
July	1	147.44
	3	156.74
	15	134.39
	21	147.69
	25	137.69
	28	142.12
	31	133.70
Aug.	3	139.35
	6	132.55
	15	146.51
	24	135.62
	29	142.58
Sept.	21	104.79
	23	117.75
Oct.	5	85.51
	9	108.96
	14	96.01
	21	109.69
	29	98.19
Nov.	9	119.15
Dec.	4	85.75
	7	92.60
	17	71.79
	19	83.09
	28	72.41
	31	79.92
1932 Jan.	5	69.85
	14	87.78
	23	77.09
	26	80.79
	29	74.19
Feb.	2	80.74
	10	70.64
	19	89.84
	24	79.57
Mar.	9	89.87
Apr.	8	61.98
	9	66.81
May	4	52.33
	7	60.01
	16	50.21
	20	55.50
June	2	43.49
	6	51.21
	9	44.45
	16	51.43
July	8	40.56
	16	45.98

	19	43.53
Aug.	8	71.49
	13	60.89
	17	70.50
	20	65.99
Sept.	8	81.39
	15	64.27
	22	76.01
Oct.	10	57.67
	20	66.13
	26	59.03
	29	63.67
Nov.	3	57.21
	12	68.87
	17	62.18
	21	64.68
Dec.	3	55.04
	15	62.89
	23	56.07
	30	60.84
1933 Jan.	3	58.87
	11	65.28
	18	60.07
	26	62.69
Feb.	6	56.65
	9	60.85
	27	49.68
Mar.	16	64.56
	31	54.90
Apr.	20	75.20
	21	68.64
	24	74.84
	28	69.78
May	11	83.61
	15	79.06
	18	84.13
	22	78.61
June	13	97.92
	17	89.10
	20	98.34
	23	91.69
July	7	107.51
	12	101.87
	18	110.53
	21	84.45
	27	97.28
	31	87.75
Aug.	10	100.14
	16	92.95
	25	105.60
Sept.	6	97.74
	18	107.68
	22	95.73
	26	100.23
Oct.	3	91.93
	9	100.58
	21	82.20
	25	95.23

	31	86.50
Nov.	21	101.94
	28	95.31
Dec.	11	103.97
	20	93.70
1934 Jan.	2	101.94
	8	96.26
Feb.	5	111.93
	10	103.08
	16	109.96
Mar.	1	101.93
	3	106.37
	8	100.78
	13	104.89
	21	98.45
	26	102.67
	27	97.41
Apr.	20	107.00
May	14	89.10
	18	96.57
	23	92.23
	28	96.33
June	2	90.85
	19	101.11
July	3	94.25
	11	99.35
	26	84.58
Aug.	2	91.12
	6	86.32
	13	92.56
	20	90.08
	25	96.00
Sept.	17	85.72
	27	94.02
Oct.	4	89.84
	17	96.36
	26	92.20
Nov.	26	103.51
	30	101.94
Dec.	6	104.23
	20	98.93
1935 Jan.	7	106.71
	15	99.54
	21	103.93
	29	100.24
Feb.	2	102.56
	6	99.95
	18	108.29
	27	101.27
Mar.	2	103.67
	18	95.95
	22	100.88
	26	98.61
Apr.	25	111.52
May	2	107.82
	16	117.30
	18	114.13
	28	117.62

1935 June 1....108.64
24....121.30
27....116.91
July 9....123.34
16....121.00
31....127.04
Aug. 2....124.28
14....128.94
20....124.97
27....129.97
Sept. 4....126.43
11....135.05
20....127.97
Oct. 1....133.19
3....126.95
28....142.08
31....138.40
Nov. 8....145.40
13....141.60
20....149.42
Dec. 2....140.38
9....145.07
16....138.91
1936 Jan. 10....148.02
21....142.77
Feb. 19....155.69
26....149.08
Mar. 6....159.87
13....149.65
26....159.53
28....154.66
Apr. 6....163.07
30....141.53
May 15....152.43
19....147.21
June 1....154.02
5....148.52
24....161.15
July 1....156.82
3....159.13
8....154.85
28....168.23
Aug. 3....164.61
10....170.15
21....160.52
28....168.02
Sept. 1....165.24
8....170.02
17....164.82
23....170.72
25....165.91
Oct. 19....178.44
26....172.16
Nov. 18....186.39
23....177.91
30....184.01
Dec. 2....179.66
15....183.30
21....175.31

31....181.77
1937 Jan. 4....176.96
22....187.80
27....182.15
Feb. 11....191.39
24....185.15
Mar. 10....195.59
22....179.28
31....187.99
Apr. 9....175.86
13....183.43
16....179.70
22....184.33
28....168.77
May 5....176.81
18....166.20
24....176.25
June 1....170.72
5....175.66
14....163.73
25....170.98
29....166.11
Aug. 14....190.38
28....175.33
31....179.10
Sept. 13....154.94
15....165.16
24....146.22
30....157.12
Oct. 6....141.63
7....150.47
19....115.84
21....137.82
25....124.56
29....141.22
Nov. 8....121.60
12....135.70
23....112.54
Dec. 8....131.15
14....121.85
21....130.76
29....117.71
1938 Jan. 15....134.95
28....118.94
Feb. 2....125.00
4....117.13
23....132.86
28....128.63
Mar. 1....131.03
12....121.77
15....127.44
31....97.46
Apr. 18....121.54
20....112.47
23....119.21
May 1....109.40
10....120.28
27....106.44
June 10....116.08

14....111.54
July 7....140.05
12....133.84
25....146.31
28....139.51
Aug. 6....146.28
12....135.38
24....145.30
29....136.64
Sept. 7....143.42
14....130.38
21....140.20
28....127.85
Oct. 24....155.38
29....150.48
Nov. 10....158.90
28....145.21
Dec. 1....150.20
5....146.44
15....153.16
21....149.06
1939 Jan. 5....155.47
13....146.03
19....149.88
26....136.10
Feb. 6....146.43
10....142.70
16....146.12
21....142.05
Mar. 10....152.71
22....138.42
27....143.14
Apr. 11....120.04
15....130.19
18....124.81
28....131.42
May 1....127.53
10....134.66
17....128.35
June 9....140.75
16....133.79
21....138.04
30....128.97
July 25....145.72
Aug. 11....136.38
15....142.35
24....128.60
30....138.07
Sept. 1....127.51
13....157.77
18....147.35
20....154.96
Oct. 4....148.73
18....155.28
20....152.55
26....155.95
Nov. 10....147.74
20....152.58
30....144.85

1939 Dec. 7....149.57
12....146.43
15....150.11
19....148.35
27....147.66
1940 Jan. 3....153.29
15....143.06
25....147.29
Feb. 5....144.69
9....150.04
26....145.81
Mar. 12....149.45
18....145.08
Apr. 8....152.09
19....145.86
24....149.45
May 3....146.42
8....148.70
21....110.61
23....117.84
28....110.51
June 3....116.44
10....110.41
18....125.31
26....118.67
28....124.42
July 3....120.14
17....123.91
25....121.19
31....127.18
Aug. 7....124.61
12....127.55
16....120.90
22....126.97
27....124.95
Sept. 5....134.54
13....127.22
24....135.48
27....131.38
Oct. 3....135.86
15....129.47
23....132.79
28....130.96
Nov. 8....138.77
28....129.13
Dec. 2....131.96
5....129.54
13....133.00
23....127.83
1941 Jan. 10....134.27
Feb. 4....122.29
10....125.13
19....117.43
26....122.90
Mar. 5....119.98
19....124.35
24....121.82
Apr. 4....125.28

23....115.33
29....117.48
May 1....114.78
13....117.93
16....115.36
21....118.45
26....115.33
June 23....125.14
July 1....122.54
9....128.77
17....126.75
22....131.10
25....127.74
28....130.37
Aug. 15....124.66
Sept. 2....128.62
11....126.31
18....130.00
25....125.33
Sept. 30....127.31
Oct. 17....117.88
24....121.69
31....117.40
Nov. 5....120.34
13....114.91
24....118.19
Dec. 1....113.06
4....117.54
10....106.87
16....112.30
24....105.52
1942 Jan. 6....114.96
12....110.10
14....113.29
22....108.30
27....111.20
Feb. 11....106.00
16....107.96
20....104.78
Mar. 3....107.16
12....98.32
18....102.73
31....99.25
Apr. 7....102.75
17....95.80
21....98.02
28....92.69
May 11....99.49
14....96.39
21....100.21
25....98.68
June 9....106.34
12....103.27
18....106.63
25....101.94
July 9....109.26
14....107.40
16....109.21

24....105.84
27....106.97
Aug. 7....104.50
19....107.88
26....105.37
Sept. 8....107.88
11....105.58
Oct. 13....115.80
16....112.71
21....116.01
28....112.57
Nov. 9....118.18
18....114.12
21....115.65
25....113.55
Dec. 18....119.76
22....118.09
28....119.96
29....117.30
1943 Jan. 4....120.82
7....118.84
Feb. 2....126.38
4....124.69
15....129.15
19....125.82
Mar. 4....131.20
10....128.49
12....131.39
22....128.67
Apr. 6....137.45
13....129.79
May 10....139.30
14....136.13
20....140.09
25....138.06
June 5....143.19
15....138.51
July 15....146.41
Aug. 2....133.87
19....138.83
23....134.40
Sept. 10....138.26
14....137.24
20....142.50
Oct. 7....136.01
20....139.21
25....137.88
28....139.74
Nov. 9....130.84
12....133.07
17....129.86
20....133.15
30....128.94
1944 Jan. 11....138.89
13....136.99
17....138.60
28....136.65
Feb. 1....137.69

1944	Feb.	7....134.10

1944 Feb. 7....134.10
17....136.77
21....135.52
Mar. 16....141.43
29....136.98
Apr. 10....139.45
25....134.75
May 12....139.38
16....138.23
June 20....149.15
24....147.12
July 10....150.88
24....145.26
Aug. 2....147.07
9....144.48
18....149.28
25....146.42
30....147.69
Sept. 7....142.53
26....147.08
28....145.67
Oct. 6....149.20
10....147.67
18....149.18
27....145.33
Nov. 10....148.39
16....145.17
Dec. 16....153.00
27....147.93
1945 Jan. 11....156.68
24....150.53
Feb. 21....160.17
26....157.45
Mar. 6....162.22
9....155.96
16....159.42
26....151.74
May 8....167.25
11....162.60
31....169.41
June 12....165.89
26....169.55
July 6....163.47
10....167.79
27....159.95
Aug. 10....166.54
21....162.28
Sept. 13....179.33
17....173.30
Oct. 18....187.55
30....182.98
Nov. 8....192.78
14....182.82
17....192.66
24....185.83
Dec. 10....196.59
20....187.51
1946 Jan. 17....205.03
21....195.52

Feb. 4....207.49
13....197.65
16....205.35
26....184.05
Mar. 9....194.70
13....188.86
26....201.85
29....198.23
Apr. 10....208.93
15....204.57
18....209.36
25....203.09
30....207.23
May 6....199.26
29....213.36
June 12....207.52
17....211.46
21....198.98
July 1....208.59
16....199.48
18....203.46
24....194.33
Aug. 14....205.01
Sept. 4....173.64
6....181.67
10....166.56
16....176.26
19....164.09
26....175.45
Oct. 10....161.61
16..:.177.05
30....160.49
Nov. 6....175.00
22....162.29
30....170.66
Dec. 3....166.20
10....177.21
13....172.57
23....178.54
27....173.88
1947 Jan. 7....179.24
16....170.13
Feb. 10....184.96
26....176.34
Mar. 6....182.48
15....171.90
24....177.61
26....174.11
28....179.68
Apr. 15....165.39
23....171.71
29....167.42
May 5....175.08
19....161.38
June 25....178.08
25....173.93
July 14....187.15
18....182.51
25....187.66

30....179.77
Aug. 1....184.38
11....178.22
15....181.58
26....176.54
Sept. 2....180.56
9....174.02
17....179.37
26....174.42
Oct. 20....186.24
24....181.55
29....184.70
Nov. 6....180.61
10....182.70
17....179.57
21....183.97
Dec. 6....175.44
22....181.78
29....177.93
1948 Jan. 5....181.69
14....176.50
17....177.59
26....170.70
Feb. 2....176.05
11....164.07
17....169.23
20....166.38
Mar: 3....169.28
17....165.03
Apr. 23....184.48
29....179.33
May 15....191.39
19....187.46
June 14....194.49
28....186.44
July 12....192.50
19....179.50
28....187.00
30....180.00
Aug. 5....184.50
11....176.50
Sept. 7....185.50
21....176.50
24....179.50
27....175.50
Oct. 26....190.50
29....186.50
Nov. 1....190.00
10....172.10
19....178.00
30....170.50
Dec. 13....178.50
17....175.50
30....179.25
1949 Jan. 3....174.50
7....182.50
17....177.75
24....182.50
27....177.50

1949 Feb.	3....180.75		23....174.50	May	5....177.25
	11....171.00		30....179.15		10....173.50
	16....175.50	Apr.	7....175.25		17....176.25
	25....170.50		18....177.50	June	14....160.62
Mar.	14....177.75		22....172.50	July	19....175.00

9-Point Chart Swings or More of the Averages

In making a chart of this kind, when the market is advancing the chart continues to move up until there is a reaction of 9 points or more. When the market is declining, the chart moves down on the line until there is a rally of at least 9 points or more, which is a reversal on the 9-Point Chart. In a few cases where the market is near the top or bottom, or an important change in trend is indicated, we record moves of less than 9 points. By studying this chart you will see how often the market moves around 9 to 10 points. The next important period to watch is moves running around 18 to 20 points, the next one around 30 points, then around 45 points and next, 50 to 52 points. A study of this record will help you in determining future trends of the main long swings on the market which is useful for long pull trading. You must learn to trade for the long pull under present income tax laws because you must carry stocks for 6 months or more.

In the prices given below "A" means an advance of a certain number of points and "D" means a decline of a certain number of points from the last high level.

1912	October	8.... 94.12				June	9.... 99.08	A 12.07
1913	June	11.... 72.11	D 20.00			December	19.... 65.95	D 33.13
	September	13.... 83.43	A 11.31		1918	October	18.... 89.09	A 23.14
	December	15.... 75.27	D 8.16		1919	February	8... 79.15	D 9.96
1914	March	20.... 83.43	A 8.16		1919	July	14... 112.23	A 33.08
	December	24.... 53.17	D 30.26				20... 98.46	D 12.77
1915	April	30.... 71.78	A 18.61			November	3... 119.62	A 21.16
	May	14.... 60.38	D 11.40				29... 103.60	D 16.02
	December	27.... 99.21	A 28.83		1920	January	3... 109.88	A 6.28
1916	July	13... 86.42	D 12.79			February	25... 89.98	D 19.90
	November	21... 110.15	A 23.73			April	8... 105.65	A 15.67
	December	21... 90.16	D 19.99			May	19... 87.36	D 18.29
1917	January	2... 99.18	A 9.02			July	8.... 94.51	A 7.15
	February	2... 87.01	D 12.17			August	10.... 83.20	D 11.31

1920	September	17.... 89.75	A	6.55
	December	21.... 66.75	D	23.00
1921	May	5.... 80.03	A	22.28
	June	20.... 64.90	D	15.13
	July	6.... 69.86	A	4.96
	August	24.... 63.90	D	5.96
1922	October	14.... 103.43	A	39.53
	November	14... 93.11	D	10.32
1923	March	20... 105.38	A	12.27
	October	27... 85.76	D	19.62
1924	February	6... 101.31	A	15.55
	May	14... 88.77	D	12.54
	August	20... 105.57	A	16.80
	October	14... 99.18	D	6.38
1925	January	22... 123.60	A	24.42
	February	16... 117.96	D	5.74
	March	6... 125.68	A	7.72
		30... 115.00	D	10.68
	April	18... 122.02	A	7.02
		27... 119.46	D	2.56
	November	6... 159.39	A	39.93
		24... 148.18	D	11.21
1926	February	11... 162.31	A	14.13
	March	3... 144.44	D	17.87
		12... 153.13	A	8.69
		30... 135.20	D	9.22
	April	24... 144.83	A	9.63
	May	19... 137.16	D	7.67
	August	24... 166.64	A	29.49
	October	19... 145.66	D	20.98
	December	18... 161.86	A	16.20
1927	January	25... 152.73	D	9.13
	May	28... 172.56	A	19.83
	June	27... 165.73	D	6.83
	October	3... 199.78	A	34.05
		22... 179.78	D	20.00
1928	January	3... 203.35	A	23.57
		18... 194.50	D	8.85
		24... 201.01	A	6.51
	February	20... 191.33	D	9.68
	March	20... 214.45	A	23.12
	April	23... 207.94	D	6.51
	May	14... 220.88	A	12.94
		22... 211.73	D	9.15
	June	2... 220.96	A	9.23
		12... 202.65	D	18.31
		14... 210.76	A	8.11
		18... 201.96	D	8.80
1928	July	5.... 214.43	A	12.47
		16.... 205.10	D	9.33
	October	1.... 242.46	A	37.36
		3.... 233.60	D	10.86
		19... 259.19	A	25.59
		22... 250.08	D	9.11
		24... 260.39	A	10.29
		31... 248.96	D	11.43
	November	28.... 299.35	A	50.59
	December	3.... 283.89	D	15.46

4... 295.61	A	11.72	
10... 254.36	D	41.25	

NOTE: This was down 44.99 from the high of November 28 at 299.35, and as 45 points is one of our rules for resistance levels this would be another reason for covering shorts and buying for a rally.

1929	January	3... 311.46	A	57.10
		8... 292.89	D	18.57
		25... 319.86	A	26.97
		30... 308.47	D	11.39
	February	1... 324.16	A	15.69
		8... 298.03	D	26.13
		13... 316.06	A	18.03
		18... 293.40	D	22.26
	March	1... 324.40	A	30.60
		6... 302.93	D	21.47
		15... 322.75	A	20.18
		26... 281.51	D	41.24
		28... 311.13	A	29.62
	April	1... 294.11	D	17.02
		5... 307.97	A	13.86
		10... 295.71	D	12.26
		23... 320.10	A	24.39
		26... 311.00	D	9.10
	May	6... 331.01	A	20.00
		9... 317.09	D	13.82
		11... 328.01	A	10.92
		13... 313.56	D	15.55
		15... 324.38	A	8.72
		16... 314.51	D	9.87
		17... 325.64	A	11.13
		23.. 300.52	D	25.12
		24.. 313.30	A	12.78
		27.. 291.80	D	21.50
		29.. 302.32	A	11.52
		31.. 290.02	D	12.32
	June	7.. 312.00	A	21.98
		11.. 301.22	D	10.78
		18.. 323.30	A	22.08
		20.. 314.32	D	8.98
	July	8.. 350.09	A	35.77
		11.. 340.12	D	9.93
		12.. 350.26	A	10.12
		16.. 339.98	D	10.28
		17.. 349.79	A	9.81
1929	July	23.. 339.65	D	10.14
		24.. 349.30	A	9.65
		29.. 336.36	D	12.84
	August	5.. 358.66	A	22.30
		9.. 336.13	D	22.53
		26.. 380.18	A	42.05
		28.. 370.34	D	9.84
	September	3.. 386.10	A	15.76
		5.. 367.35	D	18.75
		7.. 381.44	A	14.09
		10.. 364.46	D	16.98
		12.. 375.52	A	11.06

1929 September 13.... 359.70 D 15.82
19.... 375.20 A 15.50
25.... 344.85 D 30.35
26.... 358.16 A 13.31
28.... 341.03 D 17.13
October 2.... 350.19 A 9.16
4.... 320.45 D 29.74
8.... 349.67 A 29.22
9.... 338.86 D 10.81
11.... 358.77 A 19.91
17.... 332.11 D 26.66
18.... 343.12 A 11.01
19.... 321.71 D 21.41
22.... 333.01 A 11.30
24.... 272.32 D 39.31
25.... 306.02 A 35.76
29.... 212.33 D 93.69
31.... 281.54 A 69.21
November 7.... 217.84 D 63.70
8.... 245.28 A 27.44
13.... 195.35 D 49.93
20.... 250.75 A 55.40
27.... 233.39 D 17.46
December 9.... 267.56 A 34.17
13.... 239.58 D 28.08
14.... 254.41 A 14.83
20.... 227.20 D 27.21
21.... 237.26 A 10.06
23.... 226.39 D 10.87
27.... 246.35 A 19.96
30.... 235.95 D 10.40
1930 January 10.... 252.91 A 14.96
18.... 243.37 D 9.54
February 13.... 275.00 A 31.63
17.... 265.29 D 9.71
19.... 273.35 A 8.06
25.... 259.78 D 13.56
March 10.... 279.40 A 19.62
15.... 268.97 D 10.43
1930 March 21.... 284.08 A 15.11
22.... 274.63 D 9.35
April 16.... 297.25 A 22.62
22.... 284.28 D 12.97
23.... 293.27 A 9.00
29.... 272.24 D 21.03
30.... 283.51 A 11.27
May 5.... 249.82 D 33.69
7.... 272.15 A 22.33
8.... 257.74 D 14.41
14.... 277.22 A 19.48
20.... 260.76 D 16.46
June 2.... 276.86 A 16.10
12.... 241.00 D 35.86
13.... 251.63 A 9.37
18.... 212.27 D 39.36
20.... 232.69 A 20.42
25.... 207.74 D 24.95
July 1.... 229.53 A 21.79

8...214.64 D 14.89
18...242.01 A 27.37
21...228.72 D 13.29
28...243.65 A 14.93
31...229.09 D 14.56
August 5...240.95 A 11.86
13...214.49 D 26.46
September 10...247.10 A 32.61
30...201.95 D 45.15
October 3...216.85 A 14.90
10...186.70 D 30.15
15...201.64 A 14.94
18...183.63 D 18.01
20...194.44 A 10.81
22...181.53 D 12.91
28...198.59 A 17.07
November 1...181.26 D 17.33
3...187.23 A 5.99
10...168.32 D 18.91
15...187.59 A 19.27
18...177.63 D 9.96
21-25...191.28 A 13.65
28...178.88 D 12.40
December 2...187.96 A 9.08
17...154.45 D 33.51
18...171.64 A 23.19
29...158.41 D 13.23
1931 January 7...175.32 A 16.41
19...160.09 D 15.23
23...172.97 A 12.88
29...164.81 D 18.16
February 26...195.95 A 31.14
March 13...175.89 D 20.06
20...189.31 A 13.42
Apr. 7...166.10 D 23.21
14...173.24 A 7.14
29...141.78 D 31.46
1931 May 9...156.17 A 14.39
June 2...119.89 D 36.28
5...138.89 A 19.00
8...127.96 D 10.93
9...138.88 A 10.92
19...128.64 D 10.24
27...157.93 A 29.24
July 1...147.44 D 10.49
3...156.74 A 9.30
15...134.39 D 22.35
21...147.69 A 13.30
31...133.70 D 14.00
August 15...146.41 A 12.71
September 21...104.79 D 41.62
23...117.75 A 12.96
October 5... 85.51 D 32.24
9...108.98 A 23.47
14... 96.01 D 12.97
24...110.53 A 14.52
29... 98.19 D 12.34
November 9...119.15 A 20.96

1931	December	17.....71.79	D 47.36
		19.....83.09	A 11.30
1932	January	5.....69.85	D 13.24
		14.....87.78	A 17.93
	February	10.....70.64	D 17.14
		19.....89.84	A 19.20
		24.....79.57	D 10.27
	March	9.....89.88	A 10.31
	May	4.....52.33	D 37.53
		7.....60.01	A 7.68
	June	2.....43.49	D 16.52
		15.....51.43	A 7.94
	July	8.....40.56	D 10.89
	August	8.....71.49	A 30.93
		13.....60.89	D 10.69
	September	8.....81.39	A 20.50
		15.....64.27	D 17.12
		22.....76.01	A 11.74
	October	10.....57.67	D 18.34
		20.....66.13	A 8.54
	November	3....57.21	D 8.92
		12.....68.87	A 11.66
	December	3.....55.04	D 13.83
1933	January	11.....65.78	A 10.24
	February	27.....49.68	D 15.60
	March	16.....64.56	A 14.78
		31.....54.90	D 9.66
	April	20.....75.20	A 20.30
		21.....68.64	D 6.56
	June	13.....97.97	A 29.33
		17.....89.10	D 12.87
	July	18....110.53	A 21.43
1933	July	21.....84.45	D 26.08
		27.....97.28	A 12.83
		31.....87.75	D 9.53
	August	25....105.60	A 17.85
	September	6.....97.74	D 7.86
		18....107.68	A 9.94
	October	3.....91.93	D 15.75
		9....100.58	A 8.65
		21....82.20	D 18.38
	December	11....103.97	A 21.77
		20.....93.70	D 10.27
1934	February	5....111.93	A 18.23
	March	1....101.93	D 10.00
		3....106.37	A 4.46
		27.....97.41	D 8.96
	April	20....107.00	A 9.59
	May	14.....89.10	D 16.90
	July	11.....99.35	A 10.25
		26.....84.58	D 14.77
	August	25.....96.00	A 11.42
	September	17.....85.72	D 10.28
1935	January	7....106.71	A 21.00
		15.....99.54	D 7.17
	February	18....108.29	A 8.75
	March	18.....95.95	D 12.34
	May	28....117.62	A 21.67

	June	1...108.64	D 8.98
	September	11...135.05	A 26.41
	October	3...126.95	D 8.15
	November	20...149.42	A 12.47
	December	16...138.91	D 10.51
1936	March	6...159.87	A 20.96
		13...149.65	D 10.22
	April	6...163.07	A 13.42
		30...141.53	D 21.54
	June	24...161.15	A 19.62
	July	8...154.85	D 6.30
	August	10...170.15	A 15.30
		21...160.52	D 9.63
	November	18...186.39	D 5.87
	December	21...175.31	D 11.68
1937	March	10...195.59	A 20.28
		22...179.28	D 16.31
		31...187.99	A 8.71
	April	9...175.86	D 12.13
		22...184.33	A 9.57
		28...168.77	D 15.56
	May	5...176.81	A 8.04
		18...166.20	D 10.61
		24...176.25	A 10.05
	June	14...163.73	D 12.52
1937	August	14...190.38	A 26.65
	September	13...154.94	D 35.44
		15...165.16	A 10.22
		24...146.22	D 18.94
		30...157.12	A 10.90
	October	6...141.63	D 15.49
		7...150.47	A 8.84
		19...115.84	D 34.63
		21...137.82	A 21.98
		25...124.56	D 13.26
		29...141.22	A 16.66
	November	8...121.60	D 19.62
		12...135.70	A 16.10
		23...112.54	D 23.16
	December	8...131.15	A 18.61
		14...121.85	D 9.35
		21...130.76	A 8.91
		29...117.21	D 13.55
1938	January	15...134.95	A 17.74
	February	4...117.13	D 17.82
		23...132.86	A 15.73
	March	31... 97.46	D 35.40
	April	18...121.54	A 24.08
		20...112.47	D 9.07
		23...119.21	A 6.74
	May	1...109.40	D 9.81
		10...120.28	A 10.88
		27...106.44	D 13.84
	July	25..146.31	A 39.87
	August	12...135.38	D 10.93
		24...145.30	A 9.98
	September	14...130.38	D 14.92
		21...140.20	A 9.82

1938	September	28...127.85	D 12.35
	November	10...158.90	A 31.05
		28...145.21	D 13.69
1939	January	5...155.47	A 10.26
		26...136.10	D 19.37
	March	10...152.71	A 16.61
	April	11...120.04	D 32.67
	June	9...140.75	A 20.71
		30...128.97	D 11.78
	July	25...145.72	A 16.85
	August	24...128.60	D 17.12
		30...138.07	A 9.47
	September	1...127.51	D 10.56
		13...157.77	A 30.26
		18...147.35	D 10.42
1939	October	26...155.95	A 8.60
	November	30...144.85	D 11.10
1940	January	3...153.29	A 8.44
		15...143.06	D 10.23
	April	8...152.07	A 9.01
	May	21...110.61	D 41.46
		23...117.84	A 7.23
		28...110.51	D
	June	10...110.41	D 7.33
	November	8...138.77	A 28.36
	December	23...127.83	D 10.94
1941	January	10...134.27	A 6.44
	February	19...117.43	D 16.84
	April	4...125.28	A 7.85
	May	1...114.78	D 10.50
	July	22...131.10	A 16.32
	December	24...105.52	D 25.58
1942	January	6...114.96	A 9.44
	April	28...92.69	D 22.27
1943	July	15...146.41	A 53.73
	August	2...133.87	D 12.54
	September	20...142.50	A 8.63
	November	30...128.94	D 13.66
1944	July	10...150.88	A 22.06
	September	7...142.53	D 8.35
1945	March	6...162.22	A 19.69
		26...151.74	D 10.48
	June	26...169.55	A 17.81
	July	27...159.95	D 9.65
	December	10...196.59	A 36.64
		20...187.51	D 9.08
1946	January	17...205.03	A 17.52
		21...195.52	D 9.51

	February	4...207.49	A 11.97
		13...197.65	D 9.84
		16...205.35	A 8.70
		26...184.05	D 21.30
	April	18...209.36	A 25.31
	May	6...199.26	D 10.10
		29...213.36	A 14.10
	June	21...198.98	D 14.38
	July	1...208.59	A 9.71
		24...194.33	D 14.26
	August	14...205.01	A 10.68
	September	4...173.64	D 31.37
		6...181.67	A 8.03
		10...166.56	D 15.11
		16...176.26	A 9.70
		19...164.09	D 12.17
		26...175.45	A 11.36
	October	10...161.61	D 13.84
		16...177.05	A 15.44
		30...160.49	D 16.56
	November	6...175.00	A 14.51
		22...162.29	D 12.71
1947	January	7...179.24	A 16.95
		16...170.13	D 9.13
	February	10...184.96	A 14.83
	March	15...171.97	D 12.99
		28...179.68	A 7.71
	April	15...165.39	D 14.29
	May	5...175.08	A 9.69
		19...161.38	D 13.70
	July	25...187.66	A 16.28
	September	9...174.02	D 13.64
	October	20...186.24	A 12.22
	July	11...164.09	D 22.19
	June	14...194.49	A 34.40
	July	19...179.50	D 14.99
		28...187.00	A 7.50
	August	11...176.50	D 10.50
	September	7...185.50	A 11.00
		27...175.50	D 10.00
	October	26...190.50	A 15.00
	November	30...170.50	D 20.00
1949	Jan. 7 &	24...182.50	A 12.00
	February	25...170.50	D 12.00
	March	30...179.15	A 8.65
	June	14...160.62	D 18.53

July 18 high 174.44 advance 13.82.

Total Moves of 9 points or More

1912, October 8, to June 14, 1949, a period of 37 years in which there were a total of 464 moves of 9 points or more. This was an Average of about one 9-point move per month. There were 54 moves recorded of less than 9 points.

From 9 to 21 points a total of 271 moves or over 50% of the total.

From 21 to 31 points there were 61 moves or about one out of 4 times.

31 to 51 total 36 moves or about one out of 8.

Moves above 51 points were only 6 and these occurred during 1929 when we had the wildest market in history.

The above figures prove that the most important trend moves run between 9 and 21 points, and these are of the greatest importance for trend indications.

Moves of less than 9 points are of minor importance and when the Averages fail to rally as much as 9 points from a low level it is a sign of weakness and indicates lower prices. The same applies in an advancing market. If the Averages react less than 9 points it is an indication that they are in a very strong position and going higher.

When the main trend turns up and the Averages advance 10 points or more under normal conditions, they should continue to advance 20 points or more from the low levels.

After a Bear Market starts and the Averages decline more than 10 points, they should continue to decline 20 points or more. After the Averages move more than 21 points the next important point to watch is 30 to 31 points from extreme high or extreme low, as only a small percentage of moves runs over 31 points, before a move of 10 points or more occurs in the opposite direction.

Examples of 30-Point Moves:

1938 March 15 high 127.50, March 31 extreme low 97.50—a decline of exactly 30 points.

1938 September 28 low 127.50, November 10 high for the year 158.75—an advance of 31.25 points.

1939 September 1 low 127.50. This was the day Hitler started the war.   ˅

1939 September 13 extreme high for the year 157.50, exactly 30 points advance.

1946 February 4 high 207½, February 24 low 184.04—a decline of practically 24 points.

1948 February 11 low 164.04, June 14 high for the year

194.49—an advance of 30.40.

1949 June 14 low 160.62—a decline of 33.87 points from 1948 high.

From these figures you can see how often a move of around 30 points calls extreme high or extreme low of that particular move. This is especially the case in normal markets. During abnormal markets such as 1928, 1929 and 1930 moves were greater than 30 points because prices were extremely high and the range in fluctuations was very wide. These were abnormal times, and you cannot expect the market under present conditions to make moves comparable to these abnormal periods.

CHAPTER VIII

MONTHS WHEN EXTREME HIGHS AND LOWS WERE RECORDED

Because stocks run according to seasonal changes and make extreme highs in certain months at the end of a Bull Campaign, or in a major or minor move, it is important to go over past records when extreme highs are made at the end of these important moves.

1881	January and June high	1923	March
1886	December	1929	September
1887	April	1930	April
1890	May	1931	July
1892	March	1932	September
1895	September	1933	July
1897	September	1934	February
1899	April and September	1937	March
1901	April and June	1938	January
1906	January	1938	November
1909	October	1939	September
1911	February and June	1940	November
1912	October	1941	July and September
1914	March	1943	July
1915	December	1946	May
1916	November	1947	February, July & Oct.
1918	October	1948	June
1919	November	1949	January

From the above, you can see that there were 35 swings, or campaigns, in the stock market between 1881 and 1949. Below we give you the months, showing how many times the top, or high prices, were reached in each month.

January—4 highs in this month.

February—4 highs in this month.

March—4 highs in this month.

April—4 highs in this month.

May—2 highs in this month.

June—4 highs in this month.
July—4 highs in this month.
August—no highs in this month.
September—8 highs in this month.
October—4 highs in this month.
November—4 highs in this month.
December—2 highs in this month.

From the above figures, you can see that out of 35 swings, 8 made tops in the month of September. Therefore, September is one of the most important months to watch for a top when a Bull Market has been running for a long period of time. The months of January, February, March, April, June, July, October and November all show 4 tops made in each month. The months of May and December show 2 tops and the month of August shows that no important Bull Campaign reached a final high in this month. These figures give you an indication of the months to watch for the endings of a major or minor Bull Campaign.

Months When Extreme Lows Were Recorded

The Bear Markets or declines in stocks culminate a greater number of times in some months than others. Therefore, it is important for you to know when these extreme low prices have been reached. We give them below:

1884	June	1914	December
1888	April	1916	April
1890	December	1917	December
1893	July	1919	February
1896	August	1921	August
1898	March	1923	October
1900	September	1929	November
1901	January	1930	December
1903	November	1932	July
1907	November	1933	February
1910	July	1933	October
1911	July	1934	July
1913	June	1937	November

1938 March	1943 November
1939 April	1946 October
1940 May and June	1947 May
1941 May	1948 July, & March—Nov.
1942 April	1949 June

From the above figures you can see that in 36 declines, or Bear Campaigns, they have culminated, or reached final bottom, in the months indicated below:

January—1 time extreme low.
February—3 times.
March—2 times.
April—4 times.
May—3 times.
June—4 times.
July—5 times.
August—2 times.
September—1 time.
October—3 times.
November—6 times.
December—4 times.

You will note that 6 Bear Campaigns have ended in November, and 5 in July. Therefore, when stocks have been declining for a considerable period of time, you would expect them to reach final lows in the months of July or November. The next months when the most lows have occurred are April, June and December. These are the next important months to watch for the end of a decline.

The months of January and September indicate only 1 out of the 36 moves. Therefore, these months are not important for the terminations of Bear Campaigns. March only shows 2 extreme lows. If a market had been declining for some time, you could expect that the possibilities were greater for the extreme low to occur in April than in March. Study the past time periods in connection with individual stocks, as well as with the industrial averages, and the public utilities averages.

Monthly High and Low Prices Each Year

It is important to have a record of when extreme High and Low prices are reached in each calendar year. Below we are giving a record of the months when the Highs and Lows were made, and after 1897 we are giving the exact date the extreme Highs and Lows were recorded:

	HIGH	LOW
1881	January and May	February, September and December
1882	September	January and November
1883	April	February and October
1884	February	June and December
1885	November	January
1886	January & December	May
1887	May	October
1888	October	April
1889	September	March
1890	May	December
1891	January & September	July
1892	March.	December
1893	January	July 26 (extreme low)
1894	April and August	November
1895	September	December
1896	April 17	August 8
1897	September 10	April 19
1898	August 26 and December 17	March 25
1899	April 4 and September 2	December 18 June 25 and September 24
1900	December 27	December 24
1901	June 3	
1902	April 18 and September 19	December 15
1903	February 16	November 9
1904	December 5	February 9
1905	December 29	January 25

1906 January 19	July 13
1907 January 7	November 15
1908 November 13	February 13
1909 October 2	February 23
1910 January 22	July 26
1911 February 4 and	
June 14	September 25
1912 September 30	January 2
1913 January 9	June 21
1914 March 20	December 24
1915 December 27	January 24
1916 November 25	April 22
1917 January 2	December 19
1918 October 18	January 15
1919 November 3	February 8
1920 January 3	December 21
1921 May 5	August 24
1922 January 5	October 14
1923 March 20	October 27
1924 November 18	May 14
1925 November 6	March 6
1926 August 14	March 30
1927 December 20	January 25
1928 December 31	February 20
1929 September 3	November 13
1930 April 16	December 17
1931 February 24	October 5
1932 March 9	July 8
1933 July 18	February 27 and October 21
1934 February 5	July 26
1935 November 8	March 18
1936 December 15	April 30
1937 March 10	November 23
1938 November 10	March 31
1939 September 13	April 11
1940 January 3	June 10
1941 January 10	December 24
1942 December 28	April 28

1943 July 15	January 7
1944 December 16	February 7
1945 December 10	January 24
1946 May 29	October 30
1947 July 25	May 19
1948 June 14	February 11
1949 January 7	June 14

Number of Times Extreme Highs Have Been Reached
January—14 highs in 69 years.
February—5 highs in 69 years.
March—5 highs in 69 years.
April—6 highs in 69 years.
May—5 highs in 69 years.
June—3 highs in 69 years.
July—3 highs in 69 years.
August—3 highs in 69 years.
September—10 highs in 69 years.
October—3 highs in 69 years.
November—8 highs in 69 years.
December—13 highs in 69 years.

From the above you can see that 14 Highs occurred in the month of January and 13 in the month of December. Therefore, when stocks have been advancing for a considerable period of time the percentage is largely in favor of Highs being reached in December or January. During the month of September, Highs were made 10 times. This is the next month to December and January and is important to watch for Top or Change in Trend when prices have been advancing for some time. The next month for Highs is November—8 having occurred. Next, March, April and May which ran 5, 6 and 5. The months of June, July, August and October only record 3 Highs each, therefore, these months are the ones when you would least expect extreme Highs to be reached.

Number of Times Extreme Lows Have Been Reached

January—9 times in 69 years.
February—10 times in 69 years.
March—6 times in 69 years.
April—6 times in 69 years.
May—3 times in 69 years.
June—5 times in 69 years.
July—6 times in 69 years.
August—2 times in 69 years.
September—2 times in 69 years
October—7 times in 69 years.
November—6 times in 69 years.
December—13 times in 69 years.

From the above you can see that the greatest number of Lows occurred in the month of December and the next in February, therefore, December and February are the most important to watch for Lows and a Change in Trend. January comes next with 9 and October—7. The months of March, April and November all show 6. April—3, August and September—2, these months showing the least number of Lows.

Considering both the High and Low months we find September, December, January and February the months when the greatest number of Highs and Lows have occurred in the past 69 years, making these months the most important to watch for a Change in Trend either way, provided prices have been advancing or declining for a considerable period of time. By checking the months when the last High and Low have occurred will help you to determine when the next Change in Trend takes place. You should also study the exact dates each month when Highs and Lows have been reached in the past. Watch around these same dates for future Change in Trend.

Dow-Jones 30 Industrial Averages Time Swings

1912, October 8, to June 14, 1949. The swings recorded are mostly the major swings when there was a rapid advance or a rapid decline in a comparative short period of time.

During this period there was a total of 292 time swings.

3 to 11 days—41 swings in this time period or about 1 in 7.

11 to 21 days—65 swings in this time period or about 1 in 4½.

22 to 35 days—65 swings in this time period or about 1 in 4½.

The duration of time periods from 11 to 35 days was 130 or more than 1/3 of the total moves, making this time period very important to watch from any extreme high or extreme low level.

Moves lasting 36 to 45 days were 31 or about one in 9½ times.

Moves of from 43 to 60 days were 33 or about one in 9 times.

Moves of from 61 to 95 days were 20 or about one in 14½ times.

Moves of from 96 to 112 days were 13 or about one in 22½ times.

Moves lasting more than 112 days were 12 or about one in 22 times.

The knowledge of these time periods will help you in using the other rules and in determining when a change in trend is due.

CHAPTER IX

JUNE LOWS COMPARISON FOR FUTURE HIGHS

1949, June 14, the Dow-Jones 30 Industrial Averages declined to 160.62, and up to this writing, July 19, 1949, have advanced above 175. Suppose June 14, 1949 this turns out to be the low level and a Bull Market starts. By comparing the previous low levels in June and what followed them, we get a line on what is possible to expect in the future.

1913, June 11 low 72.11. September 13 high 83.43, an advance lasting 3 months.

1914, March 20, high 83.49, a Double Top against September 13 high. This was an advance of 9 months from the low in June, 1913. The main trend turned down from March, 1914 and in June, the price was 81.84, slightly lower than the Double Top. From this level the decline followed ending in a panic in December, 1914 with the Averages down to 53.17.

1921, June 20, low 66. This was the First Bottom in a Bear Market.

1921, August 24, low 64. This was Final Low, and a Bull Market started.

1923, March 20, high 105.25. Up 41 points in 21 months. This ended the First Section of the big Bull Market which lasted until 1929.

1930, June 25, low 208. This was a low in the first year of a Bear Market, and a Bull Market could not be expected to start.

September 10, high 247, up 39 points in 77 days. This was only a Rally in a Bear Market.

1937, June 14, low 163.75.

August 14, high 190.50, up 36.75 in 61 days. This was only a Rally in a Bear Market as the Bull Market had ended in March, 1937.

1940, June 10, low 110.50.

November 8, high 138.50. An advance of 28 points in 147 days. This was a Rally in a Bear Market. After this there were no more important low levels in June until June 14, 1949, which was a decline of one year from June 14, 1948.

By using the above Time Periods when lows were made in June, the most important one to consider would be the low in June, 1921 because it was at the end of a Bear Market which had lasted for about 20 months. Therefore, adding this same Time Period from 1921 to 1923 to June 14, 1949, we get March 14, 1951 as a possible time that a Bull Market would run. Assuming that from June 14, 1949 we would only get a Rally in a Bear Market, then the Time Period would run out August 14 and 31 and December 27. The other Time Periods would run out in April, 1950 and in June, 1950, which compares with previous Time Periods.

1945, July 27, last low to July 27, 1949, 48 months.

August 27, 1949, 49 months, the same time as from 1938 to 1942 lows and from April, 1942 to high in May, 1946.

July 27, 1949 will be very important for a Change in Trend, and if the trend is up at that time, or the trend turns up soon after that time, prices should go very much higher.

1938, November 10, high 158.75. Prices made Final Low April 28, 1942. This was approximately 42 months between the extreme high and low. In 1945 the Averages crossed 158.75 after having remained below this level for six years and three months. They have now remained above the level of 158.75 for a period of 50 months. Therefore, breaking below the 160 level now would indicate considerably lower prices due to the long period of time which has elapsed.

Considering that the Averages reached extreme high May 29, 1946 and now for a period of 37 months have remained in a range of 53 points and have not broken below the low levels which were recorded on the First Decline to October 30, 1946, a period of five months, should the Averages advance and get into a strong position after holding above this low level for such a long period of time, it could mean a prolonged advance and very much higher prices.

Anniversary Dates

My object in writing this book "45 Years in Wall Street" is to give you some new and valuable rules on Time Periods which will help to guide you in determining high and low prices in the future. If you study and apply these rules, they will be very valuable to you in the future.

In my research work I have discovered that stocks make an important Change in Trend in the months where they have reached extreme high and low. These are what I call anniversary dates, and these important dates should be watched each year for important Changes in Trend.

1929, September 3, a record all time high.

1932, July 8, the lowest level for the Averages since 1897, making these two dates important to watch each year for Change in Trend. The record below proves the value of these dates.

1930, September 10, last high before a Big Decline.

1931, August 29, a Big Decline started. This was just five days before September 3, the anniversary date.

1932, July 8, extreme low.

1932, September 8, high of First Rally in Bull Market.

1933, July 18, high for the year. September 18, high of Secondary Rally, from which a decline followed.

1934, July 26, low for the year. September 17, the last low from which advance started.

1935, July 21, made new high for the move. Reacted to August 2 from which the advance continued.

1935, September 11, high of the year up to that time. Decline to October 3, then crossed September 11 highs and continued up.

1936, July 28, high for the year up to that time, reacted and then continued to advance.

1936, September 8, high, reacted on September 17, and then continued up.

1937, July, no important Top or Bottom.

1937, September 15, last high of a Rally before a Big

Decline followed.

1938, July 25, high for a big reaction. September 28, last low before a big advance.

1939, July 25, high for a reaction to September 1.

1939, September 1 low, September 13 high of a 30 point advance.

1940, July 3, last low before a 20 point advance. September 13, last low before an advance to November 8.

1941, July 22, high of last Rally. September 18, last high before a Big Decline.

1942, July 9 and 16, last high for a reaction. September 11 last low before a big advance.

1943, July 15, high for a 13 point decline. September 20, high for a decline to November 30.

1944, July 10, high for a reaction to September 7.

1944, September, last low for a big up swing.

1945, July 27, last low, 159.95. This low has not been broken up to the time of this writing, July 2, 1949.

1945, September 17, low before a big up swing.

1946, July 1, last high before a big decline.

1946, September 6, top of a small rally, then declined to October 30.

1947, July 25, last high before a decline. September 9 and 26, last lows before an advance to October 20.

1948, July 12, last high before a decline to September 27.

1948, September 27, last low. Market rallied to October 26.

1949, Watch July 8, 15, 25, 28 for important changes.

September 2 to 10, 15 and 20 to 27. Important to watch for Changes in Trend.

Watch these anniversary dates every year and also watch the other dates when extreme highs and lows have been recorded, like March 8, 1937, March 31, 1938, April 28, 1942, May 29, 1946 and so on. If you put in time studying and comparing Time Periods and at the same time follow all the other rules, you will find it of great value in determining the Changes in Trend in the future.

When important news is announced, such as the beginning of war, the ending of wars, the dates of the inauguration and election of presidents, it is important to consider the price of the Averages of the individual stocks at the time of news developments and whether the trend is already up or down and the change that follows these important news dates.

1914, July 30, the starting of war. Dow-Jones Industrial Averages 71.42. December 24, extreme low 53.17.

1915, April 30, high 71.78, up to the level where prices were when war broke out. There was a reaction to May 14, low 60.38. June 22, Averages again at 71.90. From this level the reaction was small to July 9, low 67.88, then crossing the high level at the time the war broke out, the advance continued on to new high levels.

1918, November 11, end of World War I. The Averages made the last high on November 9 at 88.07 and crossed this high for the first time in March, 1919 and advanced to a new high of 119.62 on November 3, 1919.

The next important war date was September 1, 1939, low 127.51, and September 13 high 157.77. We are giving the resistance levels that have occurred around 127 to 130.

1939, August 24, 128.60. September 1, 127.51.

1940, August 12, high 127.55. September 13, low 127.32. December 23, low 127.83.

1941, July 27, low 126.75. September 30, high 127.31.

1943, February 2, low 126.38. March 22, low 128.67. April 13, last low 129.79. April 30, last low 128.94. A big advance followed.

There is always a reason why the Averages make high or low levels so many times around the same price. It is because there are certain percentage points around these levels.

1896, low 28.50. Add 350% gives 128.25.

1921, low 64. Add 100% gives 128.

1929, high 386.10. 1/3 gives 128.70.

1929, high 386.10 to 40.56, 1932 low, 1/4 of range gives 126.70.

1932. low, 40.56 to 213.36, 1946 high, 1/2 gives 126.96.

1937, high 195.59. 2/3 gives 130.32.

1937, high 195.59 to 97.46 low in 1938, 1/3 gives 130.17.

1942, low, 92.69 to 1937 high, 195.59, 3/8 gives 130.40.

There were 8 resistance levels or percentage points around these levels and the market made important tops and bottoms 11 different times around these levels. This shows you the importance of calculating percentage points and resistance levels from each important high or low level.

Resistance Levels 193 to 196

1929, November 13, low 195.35.

1931, February 24, high 196.96.

1937, March 10, high 195.59.

1948, June 14, high 194.49.

Four important tops and bottoms around these levels. The following are the reasons:

1929, high, 386.10, 1/2 gives 193.05, a very important resistance level.

1921, low, 64, add 200% gives 192.

1930, April 16, high 297.25 to 92.69, low in 1942, 1/2 gives 194.97.

1932, low 40.56 add 375% gives 192.66.

1945, July 27, low 159.95 to 213.36, May 29, 1946, 2/3 gives 195.56.

1939, September 1, low 127.51 add 50% gives 191.26.

1939, low 127.51 to 92.69, low in 1942, add 200% of the range gives 197.15.

1945, March 26, low 151.74. This was the last low before the Averages advanced to new high levels for that move.

Final high 213.36, 2/3 of the range gives 192.74. This gives 8 important resistance levels and shows why Averages have made 3 important high levels and 1 low level around these prices. Should the bull market continue in 1949 or in 1950 and cross 196 and close above these levels, it will be an indication for higher prices and the next important resistance level.

Start of Japanese War December 7, 1941

The Japanese attacked at Pearl Harbor on December 7, which was Sunday. On December 6 the low on the Dow-Jones Averages was 115.74 and the close 116.60. December 8, the high was 115.46. Prices never sold higher until extreme low of 92.69 was reached April 28, 1942. Therefore, the high of December 8 was an important point and when the Averages crossed it, it was an indication of much higher prices.

1943, October 13, high 115.80, at the low of December 6 and the high of December 8, 1941. On October 28, 1943, low 112.57, only 3 point reaction in 15 days, indicating strong up trend.

1943, November 9, high 118.18. The Averages had crossed the high price of December 8, 1941 indicating higher prices. A reaction followed to December 24, low 113.46, not 5 points decline in 45 days and not 3 points under the prices when the war started. This was an indication of good support and higher prices followed. The advance continued, and in February, 1945 the Averages crossed 127.51, the low of September 1, 1939, when the German war started.

1945, May 6, the German war ended, and the Averages continued to move up. June 26, high 169.15. This was over 10 points above the high of 1938 and had crossed all of the resistance levels between 158 and 163, a definite indication of higher prices.

1945, July 27, low 159.95, down less than 10 points in 31 days and holding at the strong resistance levels indicating higher prices.

1945, August 14, the Japanese war ended. The last low had occurred on August 9 with the Averages at 161.14, making 159.95 and 161.14 important support levels because they occurred at the end of the war with prices above the 1938 high levels, where they have held for 3 different declines without reaching 160. These examples are given to prove to you the importance of figuring resistance levels and percentage points from all important tops and bottoms in order that you can determine where the next important high or low level is likely to occur. Use all of the time rules, the 3 day chart and the 9 point chart to help you in determining the time and the price for future buying and selling levels, applying all of the rules to the individual stocks as well as to the Averages.

Resistance Levels 158 to 163

The records prove that these levels are very important for tops and bottoms as shown by extreme high and low levels.
1937, June 14, low 163.75.
1938, November 10, high 158.90.
1939, September 13, high 157.77.
1945, March 6, high 162.22.
1945, July 27, low 159.95.
1946, October 30, low 160.49.
1947, May 19, low 161.38.
1949, June 14, low 160.62.
A total of four highs and four lows around these levels. The last three important bottoms from 1946 to 1949 occurred around these levels at which the market received support and rallied each time. Below we give the percentage points showing why there was support or buying and resistance or selling around these levels. There is always a mathematical proof of why bottoms and tops occur so many times around the same level.
1896, low 28.50 to 386.10, high in 1929, 3/8 of the range gives 162.60.
1921, low 64 add 150% gives 160.
1932, low 40.56 to 195.59, high in 1937, 3/4 of the range gives 156.84.
1932, low 40.56 add 300% of the base or low gives 162.24.
1932, September 8, high 81.39, add 100% gives 162.78.
1933, October 21, low 82.20. Add 100% gives 164.40.
1938, March 31, low 97.46 to 1937 high, 195.59. 5/8 of the range gives 158.90, the exact high point of November 10, 1938.

1939, September 1, low 127.51 to 92.69, low April 28, 1942. This was the range between the starting of the war and the extreme low afterward. The decline was 34.82. Add this to 127.51 gives 162.33.

1945, March 26, low 151.74 to 213.36, extreme high. $\frac{1}{8}$ of this range gives 159.47.

1946, high 213.36. 25% of this price gives 160.02.

This shows 10 resistance points and proves why the market has made high and low levels for 8 times around these prices. The fact that June 14, 1949 the Averages reached this level for the third time and up to this writing, July 18, have rallied to 174.40 indicates that they are in strong position, but should they ever close below 160, it will be a sure indication for lower prices because it will be the fourth time, and based on our rule, prices should continue on down.

CHAPTER X

VOLUME OF STOCK SALES ON NEW YORK STOCK EXCHANGE

With Review of Bull and Bear Markets

These sales are a continuation from New Stock Trend Detector, page 81, and brings the sales up to June 30, 1949.

The bull market which started July 8, 1932, continued to March 10, 1937, with the Averages up 155 points.

1936, the volume of trade continued heavy, the months of January and February showing the greatest volume. The total volume of sale for the year 1936 was 496,138,000.

1937. The volume was heavy for the first 3 months. The month of January showed the largest volume for the year. After the decline started in March the volume decreased to 17,213,000 in August. On the big break in October the volume ran over 51 million. The total for the year 1937 was 409,465,000, much less than 1936.

1938. Final low was reached March 31, a little over one year from the top of 1937. The total volume for this bear campaign was 311,876,000.

April, 1938, to November 10, 1938. Prices advanced 61 points in this minor bull market, and the total volume was 208,296,000. In the month of October the volume of sales was 41,555,000, the largest of the year and the greatest of any month since March, 1937. This was an indication of top and indicated that the public was buying heavily on the advance. The averages reaching the exact resistance level as explained in the new book "45 Years in Wall Street."

From the high of November, 1938, prices declined to April 11, 1939, down 39 points. The volume on this period was 111,357,000. The volume in March, 1939, was 24,563,000, and in April the volume decreased and reached the lowest of the year in June.

May, 1939, to September, 1939. A total advance of 37 points. Total volume for this period was 117,432,000. The war started on September 1 and the advance from September

1 to 13 amounted to 30 points. The volume during September was 57,089,000. This was the greatest of any time since January, 1937, and indicated that the public was buying stocks heavily on the advance, and that the insiders were selling. Prices failed to cross the high of November 10, 1938, an indication of top, and a selling level. Large volume always tells of the top.

September, 1939, to April 28, 1942. The averages declined 64 points. The total volume was 465,996,000. The volume continued to decrease during 1940 and 1941. From a total of 496,138,000 in 1936, the volume in 1941 was only 170,604,000 indicating that liquidation was about completed. During February, March and April, 1942, the volume was around 8 million shares and slightly lower. This indicated complete liquidation and that the market was laying the foundation for higher prices.

1942, May to August. The volume continued to average below 8 million shares per month, indicating small buying in a liquidated market. Later in the year the volume increased, but the total for the year 1942 was the lowest in many years, only 125,652,000.

1943. There was a big increase in volume, 278 million. 1944 was 263 million.

The market continued to advance in 1945, and the total volume was 375 million, the largest of any year since 1938. This enormous volume indicated that the bull campaign was nearing the end.

1946, January. Sales 51,510,000. This was the largest sale for any month since March, 1937, and indicated that the top was near. After the high in the early part of February, the Averages only advanced 5 points higher to final high May 29, 1946.

A bull campaign was begun on April 28, 1942, and ended on May 29, 1946, with an advance of 120 points. The total volume for this period was 1 billion and 179 million. The fact that the volume had increased enormously in the last year of the advance indicated the end of the bull market.

1946, June to October 30. The Averages declined 53

points on a total volume of 136,955,000. This was a big decline in a short period of time, and the volume ran around 20 million for June, July and August.

In September when the market was breaking rapidly, the volume was over 43 million, and in October when the bottom was reached, the volume was 30 million. After that the volume continued to run small.

October 30, 1946, to February, 1947, a total advance of 27 points. Volume of sales a little over 100 million shares.

1947, March to May 19. Market declined 27 points on a volume of 60,576,000. During May when low was reached, the volume was down 20 million, showing that liquidation was not very heavy.

1947, May 19 to July 25. The Averages rallied approximately 28 points. The total volume 42,956,000. The volume in July was 25,473,000, the largest for any month in the year, indicating that the public was again buying on top, and a reaction was in order.

July 25, 1947, to February 11, 1948. The Averages declined about 25 points. Total volume was 139,799,000. The volume during February was under 17 million, the smallest for several months. The market became very dull and narrow at this time and was of small volume indicating there was no heavy selling pressure, and a rally was due, especially as the Averages were holding higher support levels than May, 1947.

February 11, 1948, to June 14, 1948, an advance of 30 points. Total volume 131,296,000. The volume in February was slightly below 17 million, and in May the total volume was 42,769,000. This was the highest volume of any month since September, 1946. This heavy volume with the Averages up to an old selling level indicated the market was making top. During the month of June, the total volume was a little less than 31 million showing that the public had loaded up in May and that buying power was decreasing on the advance.

June 14, 1948, to June 14, 1949. The Averages declined around 34 points. Total volume was 246,305,000.

In February, 1949, the volume again dropped to around 17 million, and in June, 1949, total volume was 17,767,000. This compared with the volume of nearly 43 million in May, 1948, another indication that the market was liquidated and with prices of the Averages down the low levels of October, 1946, and the lows of May, 1947, indicated a buying level. You will note that in 1947 the total volume of sales was 253,632,000, and in 1948 the total volume was 302,216,000, and the biggest percentage of this volume occurred on the advance from February to June.

The first six months of 1949 the total volume was 112,403,000. This is much less than one-half the total volume of 1948.

Should the market advance during the balance of 1949, the volume will probably increase and by the end of the year be as great as 1948.

Remember it is always important to study the volume of sales monthly and weekly and use the volume in connection with all of the other rules.

MONTHLY AND YEARLY VOLUME OF SALES ON NEW YORK STOCK EXCHANGE

(000 omitted)

	1936	1937	1938	1939	1940
Jan.	67,202	58,671	24,154	25,183	15,987
Feb.	60,884	50,248	14,525	13,874	13,472
Mch.	51,107	50,346	22,997	24,563	16,272
Apr.	39,610	34,607	17,119	20,245	26,693
May	20,614	18,549	13,999	12,934	38,965
June	21,429	16,449	24,368	11,967	15,574
July	34,793	20,722	38,771	18,068	7,305
Aug.	26,564	17,213	20,733	17,374	7,615
Sept.	30,873	33,853	23,825	57,089	11,940
Oct.	43,995	51,130	41,555	23,736	14,489
Nov.	50,467	29,255	27,926	19,223	20,887
Dec.	48,600	28,422	27,492	17,773	18,397
Totals	496,138	409,465	297,464	262,029	197,596

	1941	1942	1943	1944	1945
Jan.	13,313	12,998	18,032	17,809	38,995
Feb.	8,970	7,924	24,432	17,099	32,611
Mch.	10,124	8,554	36,996	27,645	27,490
Apr.	11,187	7,588	33,554	13,845	28,270
May	9,669	7,231	35,049	17,229	32,025
June	10,462	7,466	23,419	37,713	41,320
July	17,872	8,375	26,323	28,220	19,977
Aug.	10,873	7,387	14,252	20,753	21,670
Sept.	13,546	9,448	14,985	15,948	23,135
Oct.	13,151	15,932	13,924	17,534	35,474
Nov.	15,047	13,436	18,244	18,019	40,404
Dec.	36,390	19,313	19,528	31,261	34,150
Totals	170,604	125,652	278,738	263,075	375,510

	1946	1947	1948	1949
Jan.	51,510	23,557	20,217	18,825
Feb.	34,095	23,762	16,801	17,182
Mch.	25,666	19,339	22,993	21,135
Apr.	31,426	20,620	34,612	19,315
May	30,409	20,617	42,769	18,179
June	21,717	17,483	30,922	17,767
July	20,595	25,473	24,585	
Aug.	20,808	14,153	15,040	
Sept.	43,451	16,017	17,564	
Oct.	30,384	28,635	20,434	
Nov.	23,820	16,371	28,320	
Dec.	29,832	27,605	27,959	
Totals	363,713	253,632	302,216	112,403

CHAPTER XI

15 PUBLIC UTILITY AVERAGES

During the Roosevelt administration the public utilities were depressed and the government did everything against them. Times have changed since President Roosevelt passed away in 1945, and the utilities now get a square deal, and their prospects look brighter. It is of interest to review the course of the Averages on the utilities from 1929 to date. (Refer to Chart in back of Book.)

1929, September High 144½. November Low 64½.

1930, April High 108½.

1932, July Low 16½. September High 36.

1933, March Low 19½. This was 3 points above the Low of July, 1932 and indicated higher prices, which followed.

1933, July High 37½. This was 1½ points above the High of September, 1932.

1935, March Low 14½. This was below the Low of 1932 and the Low of 1933, and liquidation had been completed at that time, and an advance followed.

1937, February High 37½. This was back to the High of 1933 where resistance could be expected.

1938, March Low 15½, one point above the 1935 Low.

1939, August High 27½. This was still below the Low of August, 1937 showing main Trend down. Prices continued to decline.

1942, April final Low 10½. The market remained in a narrow trading range for several months and finally crossed the High of June, 1942 in October, 1942 showing Up Trend. The advance continued and in 1945 the averages crossed the High of 1939 and continued to advance crossing the Highs of 1933 and 1937.

1946, April, final high 44½. This was exactly the same price as the last high in February, 1932, a natural resistance level.

1946, October Low 32½. 1947, January High 37½.

1947, May Low 32. July High 36¼.

1948, February Low 31½, one point under the Low of October, 1946, but back to the same Lows of August, 1945.

1948, June and July High 36½, back to the High of July, 1947.

1948, November and December Low, 32½, making a Higher Bottom than February, 1948.

1949, April and May High 36½, back to the old Top Level.

June 14 Low 33.75. This was a much higher Bottom than December, 1948, showing good support. As long as the Averages hold above 33, they are in position to go higher, and when they cross 36½ will be in a stronger position and closing above 38, which is above 1947 Tops, will be still stronger and will indicate 44½, the 1946 High. The public utilities are in a stronger position than the Rails and also in a stronger position than the industrial Averages. This group of stocks is in position to lead the advance in the next Bull Market. The public utility Averages would have to break the Bottom at 31½ to indicate Lower.

August, 1949, will be important for a change in Trend in the Averages and if they have crossed Top and show Up Trend at that time, they might continue up into the spring of 1950.

Barron's Air Transport Averages

This group of stocks is definitely one of the groups for leaders in the future, and each individual company should be studied in making long pull investments in it. The review of Air Transport Averages is important and gives an indication of the future trend of air lines.

1937, January High 27¾. 1938, March Low 7½.

1940, April High 34½. 1942, April Low 13½.

1943, July High 43½. 1943, December 32½.

In December 1943 holding just below the High Level of April, 1940 shows that they were in strong position, and a rapid advance followed.

1945, December High 91½. 1947, January Low 37½.

1947, April High 46½. 1947, December Low 30.

This was below the low of December, 1943 and indicated higher prices and lower prices later.

1948, April High 39¼. 1948, November Low 25½.
1949, March Low 25¾. 1949, June Low 32.09.

Holding above the low of November, 1948 indicated strength and a rally to follow.

It is interesting to review the progressive Bottoms that these Averages have made over the past few years.

1938, Low 7½, 1942 Low 13½, 1948 Low 25½, and up to this writing, June, 1949 Low 32.09, making progressive or Higher Bottoms over a series of years which is an indication of higher prices later. It is the writer's opinion that the air lines will lead the next Bull Market. Among those that I consider best for future leaders are American Airlines, Pan American Airways, Northwestern Airways, Eastern Airlines and Transcontinental and Western Airlines. If I should have to select two that I consider the very best I would select Eastern Airlines and Pan American. These companies are well managed and have shown good earnings throughout all the years, and will be future leaders. It is my opinion that in the not distant future there will be a merger of several of the big airlines with the weaker lines, and eventually there will be three or four strong companies that will control all the business in the country. When this takes place the earnings will increase and the airlines will make rapid progress and those who buy airline stocks and hold them should get a substantial increase on their investment.

Stocks With Small Number of Shares

During the past years when Bull Markets have occurred, stocks with a small number of shares outstanding have had substantial advances, greater in proportion than corporations with a large amount of shares outstanding. It requires less money to buy up the controlling supply of stocks of this kind, and therefore, when they become scarce it does not require so much buying power to bring about an advance.

Joy Manufacturing Company

This is an old and substantial company. It is well managed and not over-capitalized. The earnings in 1949 are running very high, and the prospects of good earnings are excellent. This company with less than a million shares outstanding and with such favorable earnings has a chance for substantial advancement in a Bull Market. We review the price swing on this stock:

1941, September High 14.

1942, August Low 7½.

1943, June and July High, 12½.

1943, December Low 9¾.

1945, May High 30¼.

1945, August Low 22¾.

1946, April High 34. October Low 18¼.

1947, October High 40½. This was the record High up to this time. The price well above the 1946 High should place the stock in a strong position.

1948, February Low 31½, still above the Low of May, 1945.

1948, June High 43½. This was a new High three points above the High of October, 1947.

1948, September Low 30½, supported at the same low level as May 1945, and one point below the Low of February, 1948.

1949, March High 40. Just under the High of 1947.

1949, June Low 31½. At the same level as February, 1948 and one point above the Low of November, 1948. As long as this stock holds above 30½ it is in position to go higher. Crossing 36½ will be in a stronger position and at any time it closes above 40½ will indicate much higher prices possibly above 43 or 43½. A stock of this kind should be bought and a Stop Loss Order placed, limiting the risk. When the Trend turns up there are possibilities of substantial profits.

CHAPTER XII

PUTS, CALLS, RIGHTS AND WARRANTS ON STOCKS

Many people do not understand what PUTS and CALLS are and how to BUY and SELL them. A CALL is an option to buy a stock at a fixed price for 30, 60, 90 or 180 days. For these options you pay a premium of anywhere from $140.00 to $250.00 based upon the price of the stock and the condition of the market. All you can lose on the option is the price you pay for the call, and it is good from the day you buy it to the day it expires. For example, suppose you buy a call on United States Steel at 22 good for six months, and pay, we will say, $140.00 for the call. Now no matter how low U. S. Steel declines in the six months, you can only lose your premium money of $140.00. But, on the other hand, should steel advance to 30 at any time, you can sell the stock at 30 and your profit will be $800.00 less the cost of the call and commission.

Another thing that you could do if you had a call on steel and you had a profit—suppose that it advanced from 22 to 26 and you thought it might not go any higher. You could sell 50 shares short against it, which would give you your money back with a small profit. Then if the stock continued to advance, you would be making money on 50 shares which you would still have long. On the other hand, let us suppose that steel declines to 23. You decide that it is low enough, and you buy in 50 shares of stock and make 3 points. Then it advances on and before the time the option runs out it is up to 30 or higher, and you still get a profit on the full 100 shares.

Another way to use puts and calls is for protection. Just suppose that you are long of United States Steel and it is selling around 22. You think it might go to 16 or 15 in the next few months, and you want to be protected. So you buy a put and pay $140.00 for the premium. In the meantime, steel declines to 16 and your loss on your long stock would only be from the price of the put where you could deliver it. In the meantime, you could buy the stock and deliver against the short sale and still have your long stock with the cost reduced.

Puts

A PUT means that you buy the privilege to deliver or sell 100 shares of stock or more at a fixed price any time during the life of the option, whether it be 30, 60, 90 days or six months. Suppose that Chrysler is selling at 50, and you think it is going lower. You buy a put at 50, good for six months. You might have to pay $187.50 or $200.00 for this. That is all you can lose. Suppose that during the six months Chrysler declines to 40. You could then buy in the stock and deliver it on the put at 50 and make 10 points less the cost of the put and your commission. You could also, if you were in Chrysler, if it declined to 45 and you thought it was low enough, buy 50 shares against the PUT. Then if the stock continued to decline you would still be making on 50 shares. If it turned around and advanced over 50, you would have 5 points profit on the stock bought against the put. This is what is called trading against PUTS and CALLS.

When you buy a put or call, it is endorsed and guaranteed by a stock exchange house, and no matter how high or how low the stock goes, you can always get delivery at the price you bought a PUT or CALL. No margin requirements are due until you make a trade and then you put up the regular margins until the stock is delivered. Any broker will give you information about buying PUTS and CALLS and the margin required at the time you make delivery or accept delivery on a PUT or CALL. PUTS and CALLS are traded in through the put and call brokers in New York. You can usually get quotations any day on almost any active stock running from 30 days to six months in advance. I consider PUTS and CALLS a profitable, safe way to trade because you can risk a small amount of money and you cannot lose more than that, while your profits are unlimited if the stock goes your way.

Rights and Warrants

Many people do not understand rights and **warrants** or how to trade in them. You can buy the warrants for a very small amount of money covering a long period of time. Some warrants at the present time run for as long as 1955.

A warrant is a right issued to buy or call for a certain number of shares of stock in a company covering a certain fixed period of time. They are the same as calls on stocks except they run for a longer period of time.

Any broker who is a member of the New York Stock Exchange will give you information on warrants and buy and sell them for you. You will find it most profitable to buy warrants in periods of depression when stocks are selling at very low levels and the warrants are also selling at low levels. At the end of a bull market the stocks will be selling at high levels, and you will have bought the warrants at low levels during the depression and can sell the stocks at high levels.

The issuance of warrants by corporations desiring to increase their stock capitalization performs the function of not only assuring the maintenance of an equitable percentage ownership, but generally acts as a device for the sale of additional securities over a period of time at a price agreeable to the management.

Warrants generally extend far into the future and, as a result, become a medium by which investors and traders in effect are trading in a call or option on the stock, with the advantage of an increased leverage which is inherent in this type of instrument.

This leverage characteristic makes warrants suitable as a speculative medium as can be seen by the wide price range as compared to the range in the common stock over a period of years. This is even more marked when considered on a percentage basis.

Some warrants are useful, also, to investors who in uncertain times desire to accumulate an investment position, providing the general level of prices increases, and who, in the meanwhile, do not desire to tie up more than a limited capital. In effect, such investors will buy a call on the stock and pay a premium for the privilege.

Large Profits on Small Risks

When you buy a warrant on any stock, all that you can lose is the price that you pay for the warrant. If the stock advances, the warrants also advance, and you make profits on the warrants when you sell them without calling for the stock or exercising your warrant.

Below we give some examples of profits which could have been made buying warrants.

Tri-Continental Corporation

This is a general management investment trust, and the stock is actively quoted all of the time. In 1941 and 1942 the warrants sold as low as 1/32. In 1936 they sold as high as 5 3/8. Should you have invested $1,000.00 in 1941 or 1942 and bought the warrants you could have bought 32,000 warrants. If you had sold them at 5 in 1946, they would be worth $160,000.00, a profit of $159,000 on $1,000.00 in 4 years time, less a small commission.

Merritt-Chapman and Scott

One of the leading contractors of the United States which equipped for all kinds of construction work and also handles construction in foreign countries. There is an active market for the common stock and it pays a dividend of $1.60 per year.

In 1938-39-40-41-42 and 43 warrants on this stock sold as low as 1/4 and 3/8. In 1946 the rights sold at 12½. A $1,000.00 investment when the rights were selling at 1/4 would have bought 40,000 warrants. Should you have sold the warrants in 1946 at 12, they would be worth $48,000.00, or a profit of $47,000.00 on $1,000.00 investment.

Atlas Corporation

This is an investment, trust and holding company.
In 1941 and 1942 the warrants sold as low as 1/4, or 25

cents a share. In 1946 they sold as high as 13⅝. $1,000.00 in 1942 at ¼ would buy 4,000 warrants. In the early part of 1946 the warrants could have been sold for 13, which amounts to $52,000.00, or a profit of $51,000.00 on an investment of $1,000.00.

The above profits are not picked out as just an exception. Warrants on other stocks of different kinds have shown as great opportunities for profit.

Below we give a list of warrants and rights actively traded in on the New York Stock and Curb Exchange. These are approximately for June 30.

Actively Traded Warrants on the New York Stock and Curb Exchange

SECURITIES	COMPARATIVE PRICE RANGE STOCKS AND WARRANTS	CURRENT PRICE
	(Date) (Price Range)	
A. C. F. Brill	1944-49	
Stock	19—2	2
Warrants (1 sh. at 12½ to 1/1/50 and at 15 to 1/1/55	11½—¾	¾
American & Foreign Power	1929-49	
Stock	199¼—¼	1⅝
Warrants (1 sh. at $25 at any time)	174—1/32	
Atlas	1936-49	
Stock	34⅜—5¾	20
Warrants (1 sh. at $25 at any time)	13⅝—¼	4⅜
Colorado Fuel & Iron	1936-49	
Stock	25⅞—4½	12½
Warrants (1 sh. at 17½ to 2/1/50) .	12½—½	⅞
Commonwealth & Southern	1930-49	
Stock	20¼—⅛	3½
Warrants (1 sh. at $30 at any time) .	6¼—1/256	1/16
Electric Power & Light	1926-49	
Stock	103½—⅝	24¾
Warrants (1 sh. at $25 at any time) .	78⅛—1/16	8¼
Hussmann-Ligonier	1945-49	
Stock ADJ for 2 for 1 split July, 1947	18½—9	10¼
Warrants (1 sh. at $8.45 to 5/15/50)	14¾—3½	4

MERRITT CHAPMAN SCOTT   **1936-49**

Stock	27¾—1¼	18⅛
Warrants (1 sh. at $28.99 at any time)	12½—¼	4½—5½

NIAGARA HUDSON   **1937-49**

Stock	16⅞—⅞	9½
Warrants (1 sh. at $42.86 at any time)	3⅜—1/32	5/32 B

TRI-CONTINENTAL   **1930-49**

Stock	20¼—⅝	6¼
Warrants (1.27 shs. at $17.76 at any time)	9—1/32	2⅛

UNITED CORP.   **1930-49**

Stock	52—3/16	3
Warrants (1 sh. at $27.50 at any time)	30⅞—1/256	⅛

WARD BAKING CO.   **1945-49**

Stock	19⅞—8¾	12
Warrants (1 sh. at $12.50 to 4/1/51 and 1 sh. at $15.00 to 4/1/55) .	9⅛—2¾	2¾

CHAPTER XIII

NEW DISCOVERIES AND INVENTIONS

During the past history of the world following each depression some new discovery or some new invention has stimulated business and progress and brought on another boom. Fulton's invention of the steam engine and Whitney's invention of the cotton gin started a new era of progress. In 1849 the discovery of gold in California brought on a wave of prosperity. From that time on, the progress of the railroads opened up the central and the western part of the United States, and great progress was made through this new mode of transportation.

The Bible tells us that old things pass away and new ones come to take their places. The canal boats and stage coaches passed away to give way to the railroad, a more rapid mode of transportation. Then came new discoveries and new inventions and the new mode of making steel, and the United States became an industrial nation and made great progress. In the early 1900's the progress and invention of the automobile revolutionized transportation and started another wave of prosperity giving employment to thousands of people. Then followed chemical discoveries and inventions, Rayon, and other new discoveries along chemical lines which aided progress and prosperity. Often when we were in the depths of a depression and things looked the worst, some new discovery or invention has brought about a revival of business and another wave of prosperity.

The invention of the airplane by the Wright brothers started another wave of prosperity and brought on increased rapid transportation which has not yet reached its height. This greatest mode of transportation of all is bringing all parts of the world closer together and uniting people for peace and business purposes. How much the airplane will do in the future to bring about greater prosperity remains yet to be seen, but its usefulness in every field of transportation is increasing day by day and its possibilities are unlimited. There is one problem with the airplane. That is, cheaper fuel and lighter fuel. This problem will no doubt be solved. When the load of fuel has come down and it becomes a pay load, air transportation, both for express, freight and passengers will become the cheapest mode of transportation in the world as well as the fastest. This will help to revolutionize business and bring on another wave of prosperity.

Atomic Power

The United States won the war in 1945 by the use of atomic power which was developed by the United States. While this atomic power caused great destruction of Japan at the cost of many lives, it shortened the war and saved many lives which would have been lost should the war have been prolonged. This great invention of power has possibilities beyond the comprehension of the average man, and it may he the very power that will solve the most difficult problem with the airplane by giving them cheap fuel and a great reduction in weight thereby making the load now carried as weight for gasoline a pay load which would increase not only the speed but increase the amount of cargo and passengers carried. It would give greater space for passengers and for cargo when the fuel is limited to a small place with greater power. There is a possibility that *atomic* power can be produced once it is perfected cheaper than any other fuel that man has ever invented. This would revolutionize air transportation and help to bring about increased prosperity. Not only *atomic* power but the power from the sun or from the air has possibilities in the future which would give cheap power and revolutionize manufacturing in many lines. This would cut the cost of production benefiting the consumer and giving him more for his dollar, therefore increasing the purchasing power because it is a well known fact that when the cost comes down the consumption increases. We can always buy unlimited amounts of anything when the price is within our means. *Atomic* power for energy holds the key to the future for cheap power and undreamed possibilities for this new discovery.

CHAPTER XIV

GREAT MARKET OPERATORS OF THE PAST

This writer recalls the panic of 1893 to 1896, when cotton sold as low as 3 cents a pound in the south, and a panic swept across the country which the people said was one of the worst in history. The price of wheat and other commodities was low, and I remember the first corner that I ever read about. The corner in wheat by Lighter in Chicago. In this campaign Lighter forced wheat from below $1.00 a bushel to $1.85 per bushel. He had a vast fortune made in paper profits, but he went broke. The old and valuable lesson that we can learn from studying the history of past large operators is what causes them to go broke after they accumulate a large fortune. In the case of Lighter, it was the unknown that caused his downfall. He did not believe that wheat could be delivered in Chicago in sufficient quantities to depress the market, but Armour, who was smarter than Lighter had reckoned on, had wheat shipped in by express cars for delivery. He broke the corner and Lighter went broke. No man gets so smart but what the unknown or the unexpected can happen and cause him to lose all the money he has made or the greater part of his fortune. Therefore, the lesson to be learned by mistakes of others is, don't make the same mistake. Most operators lose their money because they lose all sense of proportion, and they have only the desire for the power that money can give and want to corner the markets. Corners force prices too high and inflicts suffering upon the consumer, and the result is that almost all of them who have tried this have gone the same way. They have gone broke.

I was in the cotton market during the Sully campaign of 1903 and 1904. Sully amassed millions of dollars in a short period of time by buying cotton. He made the mistake of all great operators of thinking that he had too much power and that he could begin to force prices higher. The result was that Sully went broke and went through bankruptcy.

Theodore H. Price, another great operator in cotton of his day, made the same mistake of buying too much and underestimating the unexpected, and he also went broke. But with due respect to his memory, it must be said that Price made one of the greatest comebacks of any man in history, and made back millions of dollars and paid his creditors dollar for dollar. Another operator who started from a few hundred dollars and amassed millions of dollars and then went broke was Eugene Scales. Why did Scales go broke in the cotton market after accumulating millions of dollars? He went broke because he had a greater desire for power and to run the market than he had for making profits and using extreme cautious judgment. A man uses one kind of judgment and caution when he starts with a very small amount of money and entirely different judgment when he amasses a large amount of money. He does not figure that the unexpected can happen. Scales was a chronic bull. He never thought the market was going to reach top, and he continued to buy cotton hoping and believing prices would go higher, until finally he went broke, and died with very little money.

Jesse L. Livermore, one of the most spectacular traders of his day, made millions of dollars in the stock and the commodity markets. He went broke several times and went through bankruptcy several times, and a few times he paid out after he had gone bankrupt. Livermore was an honorable man and believed in paying debts even after he had been relieved through the courts of bankruptcy. I first met Livermore in 1908 and again in 1913 when he was trading through the firm of Murray Mitchell and Company, which failed, and I lost all of my money. In 1917 when Livermore came back and made a fortune, he not only paid back my proportionate part of money which I lost through the Mitchell failure, but paid everyone else. This was an honorable thing to do, and because of Livermore's honor and honesty, in 1934 when he was broke, I backed him and got other people to raise money and back him. Livermore came back again and made money. But Livermore's one weak point was that he never studied anything, except how to make money. He never studied the rules for keeping money. He had the greed and the desire for power, and when he got a large amount of money, he could not trade conservatively. He tried to make the market go his way instead of waiting until the market was ready to follow the natural trend. Livermore, after making the many fortunes, committed suicide and died practically broke. Why did a man who made so many millions of dollars as Livermore not keep them? It is because each time he had the same greed, the same desire for power, to be a great man and run the market. He wanted to rule, and he did not figure that the unexpected could happen, which it did and always will, and the result was that he lost his money.

Doctor E. A. Crawford, another great character and a great trader, made and lost several fortunes. He started again with a few thousand dollars in 1932 and probably made money faster than any other operator who was ever in the market. It is reported that at the height of the market in 1933 that he had accumulated a paper profit anywhere between 30 and 50 million dollars. He was buying all food products. Not only in the United States, but in foreign countries he was heavily involved in the stock market. Dr. Crawford failed July 18, 1933, and all commodity markets smashed wide open on his failure. Why did a man who could amass so many million dollars as this go broke? Simply because he did not figure that the unexpected could happen and that somebody could sell more grain and commodities than he could buy. He figured that prices were going to continue up without any reaction, which they always have to have. The result was he kept on buying until the fatal day came and he was forced to sell. He had thrown caution to the winds in buying, forgotten all the rules which he used in making money when he started on a small amount of capital, and the result was that without obedience to the rules of finance there could be but one result. Failure. He, like all other operators, made the great mistake of overtrading. This is the greatest sin of all speculative operators—overtrading, throwing caution to the winds and not figuring that the unexpected can happen. Last but not least of all of the great market operators was Jordan of New Orleans, who, it is reported, started with $300.00 a few years before 1946 and by operating in the cotton market accumulated many millions of dollars. Jordan went the way of all operators. He went broke. Why? Because he believed that cotton would keep on going up. He could not see any top, and he did not take profits. I am told that Jordan talked about cotton going as high as it went in the Civil War, $1.89 a pound. He forgot or did not know the rules of supply and demand. He continued to buy until he could buy no more. He had a great following. The public was buying. So finally, when the day came to try to sell, there were no buyers, and everybody became sellers. The collapse came from a high of 3928 for October Cotton on October 9, 1946 prices declined in less than one month's time to 2310 on November 7, 1946. Not only Jordan lost all of his fortune, but his followers lost millions of dollars and even the United States Government could not stop the decline in the cotton market. The Government and members of exchanges and other operators were forced to call in Anderson and Clayton and get them to take over the contracts of cotton held by Jordan and his followers in order to save the day. Jordan, like all of the other great operators, had not studied the market to know when prices were at abnormal levels. If he had carefully studied the prices of previous wars, especially the World War when cotton went to 43 cents a pound, July option selling at 4375, he would have known that prices were at abnormal levels. Again if he had reviewed the year 1923, he would have found that prices made high on November 30 around $37\frac{1}{2}$ cents, and should have known by these records that when prices advance anywhere between $37\frac{1}{2}$ cents and 39 cents a pound that they were at abnormal levels brought about by war conditions which always create abnormal prices. Had he considered well these facts, he would have started selling out long cotton in time to protect his profits and could have gone short and made another vast fortune. Had he understood the rules and fundamental principles of the market, he would have known the small gain that the cotton prices made in the last few weeks indicated that somebody was selling in almost unlimited quantities, and he should have started to sell at the time when he could have gotten out. But man's greatest enemy, hope, kept him holding on until the disaster came, and he went down the same as all the others because the unexpected happened, and someone was able to sell more cotton than he could buy. He was in bad company, the public was with him on a large scale. When he tried to get out, everybody else was trying to get out.

What can the ordinary man, speculator, investor or trader, learn from the history of great operators who have amassed millions of dollars and have lost them? He can learn the lesson of why they lost it, and what rules they failed to follow, and not do the same things that they did. Then he has a chance to make money and keep it. The greatest thing he must learn, and the most important, is not to overtrade. The next thing he must learn to do is to use *stop loss orders*, protecting both his principal and his profits by an automatic *stop loss order*. He must trade on facts eliminating both hope and fear, the trader's greatest enemies. If a man buys and holds on on hope, eventually he will sell when he fears the worst, and then it is too late.

Facts are stubborn things, but they must be faced and hope must be eliminated by any man who expects to make success by trading in stocks or commodities. A man must remember that the trend of markets change and he must change when the trend changes. He must learn the rules that have worked in the past and apply them in the market in the future in order to make a success.

We have reviewed the history of great market traders who have made millions of dollars and lost them. There must be exceptions to all rules. There are men who have made the money and kept it by following the right rules of finance.

Who are some of these great market operators who made the money and kept it? Bernard Baruch is one. He is an old man, retired and still worth millions of dollars, the greater part of it which he made out of investments and speculations in the stock market. Ben Smith, another operator of recent years, made the money and kept it. Bert Castles, another large operator, made money and kept it and died with it. How did Castles do it? When he bought he always placed a *stop loss order* on stocks not more than 5 points from the price at which he bought or sold. This limited his loss if he was wrong. When he was right, he let his profits run until he had a definite reason to cash in.

Successful investors have definite plans and rules, and follow them. If you expect to succeed, you must learn the right rules first; then follow them.

I could mention many more successful investors and traders who made millions of dollars and have kept it. What different rules did they follow from the rules followed by the plungers who made millions and then lost it? These wise operators, speculators or investors, if you please to call them that, were men who followed definite rules of finance. They learned how to determine the trend of stocks and commodities and bought at the right time. They were not hogs. They knew when to take profits. They knew that the unexpected could happen. They did not overtrade, and they sold when everybody else was buying and bought when everybody else was selling. This could not be done by ordinary human judgment or guess work. They had to follow well formulated rules, secure all the information possible and use the proper caution and not overtrade. This is the reason that they made a success and did not go broke. It is well for any trader to remember that when he makes a trade, he can be *wrong.* Then how can he correct that *mistake?* By putting on a *stop loss order* and taking a small loss. Unless a man knows the risk he is going to take and how much of his capital he can risk on a trade, he should never start speculating. Because without knowing these fundamental rules, sooner or later the unexpected will happen and he will go broke. It is not my object in writing this book after 45 years experience, to paint a rosy picture of an easy way to get rich, because there is no easy road to riches. My object is to tell you the truth and give you practical rules that will work if you put in the time to study and have the patience to wait for opportunities to *buy* and *sell* at the *right time*, you can make a success. Every man takes out of life just exactly according to what he puts in. We reap just what we sow. A man who pays with time and money for knowledge and continues to study and never gets to the point where he thinks he knows all there is to know, but realizes that he can still learn, is the man who will make a success in speculation or in investments. I am trying to tell you the truth and give you the benefit of over 45 years of operating in stocks and commodity markets and point out to you the weak points which will prevent you from meeting with disaster. Speculation can be made a *profitable profession.* Wall Street can be beaten and there is money operating in commodities and the stock market if you follow the rules and always realize that the unexpected can happen and be prepared for it.

CHAPTER XV

STOCKS LIOUIDATED

While the Dow-Jones 30 Industrial Averages have declined only 25% from the 1946 Highs, many individual stocks are down 75 to 90% from the Highs recorded in 1945 and 1946. The stock market discounts business six months or more in advance. Can stocks go up while a business depression is on? They can. It has happened in the past and it can happen again.

Airline Stocks

This group of stocks has been liquidated more than almost any other group. The air industry is a growing industry. It is not going out of business, and airline stocks will go up and sooner or later have sensational advances. They *will* become future leaders.

The following are the High and Low prices for recent years:

American Airlines	1945 High 95½	1948 Low	6
Bell Aircraft	1946 High 35½	1948 Low	10¾
Bendix Aviation	1945 High 63	1949 Low	26
Braniff Airlines	1945 High 37½	1948 Low	6
Eastern Airlines	1945 High 134	1949 Low	13
(1946 High 31½ after stock dividend)			
National Airlines	1945 High 41¾	1938 Low	4
Northwest Airlines	1945 High 63¾	1949 Low	7
Pan American World Airways	1946 High 29	1948 Low	8
Trans-World Airways	1945 High 79	1948 Low	9½
United Airlines	1945 High 62½	1948 Low	9½

Among the very best to buy are Eastern Airlines, Pan American and United Airlines.

The following stocks have declined to very Low Levels and show possibilities of advancing in the next Bull Market:

Gimbel Bros.	1946 High	$73\frac{3}{4}$	1949 Low	12
Lockheed	1946 High	$45\frac{1}{2}$	1947 Low	$10\frac{1}{2}$
			1949 Low	$16\frac{1}{2}$
Martin, G. L.	1946 High	$47\frac{3}{4}$	1949 Low	7
Montgomery Ward	1946 High	104	1949 Low	$47\frac{1}{2}$
Pure Oil	1948 High	42	1949 Low	$24\frac{5}{8}$
Philco Radio	1948 High	$46\frac{1}{2}$	1949 Low	$25\frac{1}{4}$
Standard Oil of New Jersey	1948 High	93	1949 Low	$60\frac{1}{2}$
Sperry	1946 High	$40\frac{1}{2}$	1947 Low	17
U. S. Rubber	1946 High	$80\frac{1}{2}$	1949 Low	33
General Motors	1946 High	$80\frac{1}{2}$	1946 Low	$47\frac{1}{2}$
	1947 High	$65\frac{3}{4}$	1948 Low	$15\frac{1}{2}$
	1948 High	66	1949 Low	$51\frac{7}{8}$

(In 1943 the Low was $48\frac{3}{4}$. The Lows have been progressively higher since that time, showing good support and unless General Motors breaks $51\frac{7}{8}$ and closes below this level it is in a position to go higher. 1947 and 1948 is a Double Top, and should General Motors ever close above 66 it will indicate very much higher.)

Special Stocks

Admiral Corporation	1945 High	$22\frac{1}{2}$	1947 Low	6
	1948 High	$22\frac{5}{8}$	1948 Low	7
	1949 High	$20\frac{1}{4}$	1949 Low	$14\frac{3}{4}$

(This company is well managed and is showing good earnings. The stock was well supported on the decline in June 1949 and shows possibilities of going higher, especially if a Bull Market develops.)

Columbia Pictures	1945 High	$45\frac{1}{2}$	1948 Low	$7\frac{1}{2}$
Consolidated Vultee	1946 High	37	1948 Low	$7\frac{3}{4}$

Columbia Gas Has been making Higher Bottoms each year

since 1942 and is in a position to go higher.

Electric Bond & Share   1946 High 26½ 1947 Low 9

This stock is in a strong position. Cash assets of the Company are much greater than the price for which the stock is selling. There is a possibility of a cash distribution of 12 and 14 dollars per share before the end of 1949. The stock is making progressively Higher Bottoms and is holding around 13¼ which is a 50% decline from the 1946 High, making this a safe, sure Buying Point. When the stock advances above 16 it will be in a very strong position and will indicate higher prices, possibly 25 to 26.

The above list of Special Stocks is in a position to become leaders in the next Bull Market. Remember, when you buy a stock, protect it with a Stop Loss Order and if it does not act right within a reasonable length of time, sell it and take a small loss.

CHAPTER XVI

CAN UNITED STATES AFFORD ANOTHER WAR?

In 1918 when we finished the World War, it was supposed to be the war that would end all wars. In 1939 Hitler started war again, and in 1941, we were forced into the war. The United States financed Russia and all of the other countries to help defeat Germany with the object that it was to end war for all times and that we were to have peace and prosperity.

What happened? Just as soon as the war was over, the United States started preparing for another war and propaganda has been circulated from time to time that sooner or later we would have to fight Russia. 15 to 16 billion dollars is being spent in 1949 in preparation for war. If we fought two wars to end wars and are now getting ready for another war, would that end war for all time? It would not; because wars have never settled anything and until men learn to settle differences without resorting to war, there can be no permanent peace. No matter who wins in war, they lose. War is a destructive, losing business. It costs the manhood of a country as well as the vital food products and necessities from manufacturing lines. The United States now has a debt of over 250 billion dollars. How can the United States afford to fight another war? Where would they get the money to finance it? Who would or who could afford to buy the bonds to finance another war? If we go into another war, it simply means complete bankruptcy and destruction of the United States. Wars are too costly. The United States is already mortgaged for more than can be liquidated, considering all government and private debts. What we need in Washington is men of vision and brains who will talk and work for peace and not waste money and prepare for war.

Why did we go to war in December 1941? Because our liberty was threatened and was insecure, we risked our lives and our resources to win a war and make our liberty secure.

We thought we were making it secure. But is it secure? And do we have the liberty that we had before the war? We do not, because the New Deal is taking the liberties away as fast as they can. The New Deal continues to talk of security. They are going to take care of people from the cradle to the grave; provide social security, provide medical treatment, provide everything. What this country needs, and the people as individuals, is not security, because security does not make progress. Security breeds defeat and worklessness. The country worked hard and risked everything when they were insecure. A man will work harder and make greater progress when he is insecure, and it is better that he is that way. If the government could provide everything for the people, which, of course, is impossible, it would then create nothing but a nation of loafers and everything would soon go to decay. The New Deal thrives on promises, promising everybody something for nothing, and the fellow who wants to get something for nothing is the man who will not give or produce. What this country needs is not more promises, but more production. The problems of this country can only be solved by more work and more saving, not by less work and more pay. If we are to have a free and independent country and retain the liberty for which our forefathers fought, then the rights for all must be equal. When our soldiers go to war, if they disobey orders or refuse to fight, they are shot down. They cannot go on a strike and refuse to fight; yet while the war was on, union labor continued to strike while our boys were risking and losing their lives. Why had union labor more right than the soldier who risks his life? He has not. The right to union labor leaders is given by politicians who have betrayed the rights of the people who elected them. Why has union labor the right to strike and cut off the necessities of life, to cause people to go hungry, cold and suffer all kinds of privations? Just because union labor leaders are trying to force business to give more pay for less work. This cannot make a prosperous country.

What caused France to lose the war? It was union labor and communism. The workers would not work and produce.

The result was France lost the war because the German people were not only willing to work, but they were forced to work and produce, and they won the war against France. Who gives to union labor the rights not enjoyed by capital or the private citizen? The law makers, who are elected by the people. They make laws to favor those whom they think can keep them in power? Is this justice? Is this liberty?

War or Peace

With our government preparing for war and talking about having to fight Russia sooner or later, war could come. If things get worse for the New Dealers, which they probably will, and they see a possibility of being defeated in 1952 they may bring on the war and then tell the people that they can't change horses in the middle of a stream and thereby try to scare the people into voting to keep them in power. What the investor wants to know is: What effect would war have on the price of stocks? It all depends upon the price stocks are selling at at the time war should start. It is my opinion that another war would be very bearish on stocks and might mean that the government would confiscate all stocks as well as other property, because with the present heavy debt it might be impossible to sell bonds to finance another war. In a case of this kind the government would have to resort to any means to obtain funds to finance a war.

Neither this country or any other country can stand another war without becoming bankrupt, and civilization could go back hundreds of years. We should all hope, pray, and vote for men who will keep us out of war.

How to Stop Wars

Wars in any country can be prevented. People have the right and have the power in their own hands to stop war. If our lawmakers can be prevailed upon to pass a law that no government can go in debt or sell bonds for war purposes, there certainly would be no war. If the government had to start a war out of its income, and not go in debt there would be no war. It has no right to go in debt, and to risk the people's lives and their money and mortgage their future. Nothing can be gained by war. This country needs to get on a cash basis and spend only its income and let that income be an excuse for cutting down government expenses.

THE GOVERNMENT CANNOT PREVENT DEPRESSION

GREAT PANIC COMING

The depression and panic will come before the New Deal goes out of office in 1953. Nothing can prevent it. Panic and depression have always followed war. The second World War cost the United States more money than any war in history. Our government debt is almost as great as the debts of all the balance of the world put together. With this burden of debt and the government expenses, how can a panic and depression be prevented? Wars have created nothing and added nothing to the value of any country. The United States has been the greatest spender and the greatest waster, and the taxpayers will be the greatest losers. I believe the Bible when it says that you shall reap just what you sow. New Dealers did not stop spending when the war ended, in fact, increased spending. They have given away tens of billions of dollars, and the result will be a panic and depression which will shake the foundation of this country and cause the voters to vote out the New Deal boys in 1952. It will be too late to do anything after the crash comes. Taxpayers have it in their power to stop this expense if they will organize and do something about it before it is too late. If New Deal spending and giving away continues as it is at the present time, it will just be a matter of a short time before the government will begin to confiscate property and everything else. Then the sons of liberty will march to fight for the liberty that they have lost in fighting wars before. The government, as Will Rogers said, never lost a war, but never won a conference.

What Will Cause the Next Depression or Panic

There will be many causes of the next great depression. England is broke as a result of the two great wars and most all of the other countries in Europe are in the same fix.

Japan, China, and India are in a bad financial condition and are likely to get worse if Communism continues to dominate China.

The United States debt is a great burden which cannot be overcome. The wasteful spending by our government has already caused irreparable damage and even if it should stop now panic would come anyway.

Foreign investors are already selling stocks in our market and have been for some time.

The investors in the United States nearly always sell in the last stages of a bear market. This causes a wide open break. In the future, as things get worse, insurance companies will have to liquidate stocks and bonds. Investment trusts will try to support stocks for a time and buy on a scale down but as conditions get worse they may get scared and become sellers in the last stages of the bear market after it has run for several years.

When the business men and investors in the United States lose confidence in the government's ability to prevent a depression then matters will get worse because business and the stock market hold up as long as people have confidence.

If the day comes, and it is not impossible, when the government can no longer support bond prices, this will be the last straw that will destroy public confidence and bring on the worst panic this country has ever seen. Effects always follow causes. The causes already exist and the government has sown the seed for another panic and depression and the cycles of business and the stock market prove that a panic is inevitable.

Future Trend of Stocks

Many economists and market experts all believe that a depression and panic is coming. Just when it will come they do not know because they do not understand time cycles. The Master Time cycle which I have used to forecast every important boom and depression or panic for more than 30 years, will in my opinion accurately forecast the next panic.

The New Dealers at Washington claim that they have the

magic formula for stopping inflation and preventing depressions and panic. The next few years will prove whether or not they can do it, because the acid test will come.

My cycle theory indicates that the business boom following the war ended in 1948 and that the trend is now down. As a rule, business has the first down swing and then a rally or a moderate up swing which fools most of the people and makes them believe that a business boom is coming again.

My study of time cycles indicates that the business depression will get worse in the last half of 1950 and in 1951 and 1952 we will run into real panicky and depressing conditions which the government will be unable to cope with. This will cause declines in stocks, bonds, commodities and everything else. Just how low stocks will go depends upon how much they rally in the next up swing and how high they are selling when the last down swing starts. Below I outline the approximate dates when changes in trend can be expected in the stock market.

There is a possibility, based on past cycles, that stocks will advance in the latter part of 1949 and continue on up into 1950. The stock market often runs six months or more ahead of business.

Outlook for 1950

1950, January 3 to 7 should be low for stocks, and the trend should turn up. The advance should continue in February with the market active.

March 18 to 22 may be top for reaction, which could run for a short period of time, possibly March 30 to 31, when a change in trend is indicated.

April. The advance should continue this month, and it is possible that final high for the year could be reached around April 25 to 30, especially if June 1949 proved to be low, this would mean that the bull wave had run 10 months, which is often the length of a short swing. Another reason is that this will be six years from April 1942 low and that the month of May and June will be 48 and 49 months from the 1946 high, making it very important for a change in trend.

June 14 to 21, important because it will be two years from the 1948 low and one year from June 14, 1949, if this proves to be extreme low. Around June 24 to 30, watch for important change in trend. The market could be bottom for a rally.

July. Stocks should advance this month even if the market is on the down trend there should be a rally in the bear market.

July 7 to 10 and 18 to 30, important for tops and a change in trend.

August. Some declines, but the market may be slow and narrow.

August 5 to 10, 14 to 18, 23 to 27 are dates for change in trend.

September. Remember this is one of the important anniversary months. You should watch for a change in trend the early part of the month and again around September 23 to October 3, which could be low for a rally. If the advance starts at this time, prices could rally up to around November 2 to 4, election time.

November 14 to 21, the time cycles indicate a decline and a possible low near the end of the month for a rally.

December. If the rally started in November, it could last to around December 15 to 20, when you should watch for top and a change in trend.

Preview of 1951 to 1953

1951 and 1952 indicate very depressing years for business and a bear market in stocks. Many stocks will go much lower than people ever dreamed they could go. The United States Government will have many difficult problems to face, and they will find it hard to solve them, as the majority of people will have lost confidence in the New Deal and their powers to prevent a panic. When once the people lose confidence, conditions get worse very fast.

The time cycles indicate a strong possibility that a Republican president will be elected in November, 1952, and it is possible that October and November, 1952 may mark the end of the bear market in stocks.

1953, January 20, a new president will take office, and if this is the Republican party, it will mean an improvement in business and starting of a new cycle. However, the cycles indicate that business is likely to be slow until April or June, and then during the summer and fall stocks will advance and business conditions will show a big improvement.

CONCLUSION

"45 Years In Wall Street" is finished. My actual experience on Wall Street dates back to 1902—47 years ago. These years have taught me my most PRECIOUS POSSESSION is TIME. The best use I can make of TIME is to use it to secure KNOWLEDGE which is more valuable than money.

In this book I have revealed some of my most valuable rules and secret discoveries never published before, in hopes that others will work and study hard to learn and apply these rules. If they do, speculation and investing will no longer be gambling but will become a PROFITABLE PROFESSION.

W. D. GANN

July 18, 1949

DOW JONES 30 INDUSTRIAL
AVERAGES
3 DAY CHART
A

8 NOV. 1940
28   2 DEC
3   15
28   10 JAN 1941
FEB 8   10
19   28
MAR 3
3 APR   24
MAY 1   29
15   5
28   21
JULY 1   25 JUNE
17   3 JULY
22
28
15 AUG   2 SEPT
11   18
28   30
17
31 OCT   24
13 NOV   5 NOV
1 DEC   23
10   4
24 DEC   16
17   6 JAN 1942
22   14
11 FEB   27
20   18
12 MAR   3 MAR
31   15
17   21
11 MAY
15   21
12   9 JUNE
25   18
16   9 JULY
24   27
AUG 7   19
25   8 SEPT
1 SEPT
14   15 OCT
28   20
18   4 NOV
25 NOV   21
22   15 DEC
29   26
7   9 JAN 1943
2 FEB
19   18
10   4 MAR
22   18
13 APR   6 APR
14   10
25   20
13   5 JUNE
2 AUG   15 JULY 1943

—134—

3 DAY CHART B

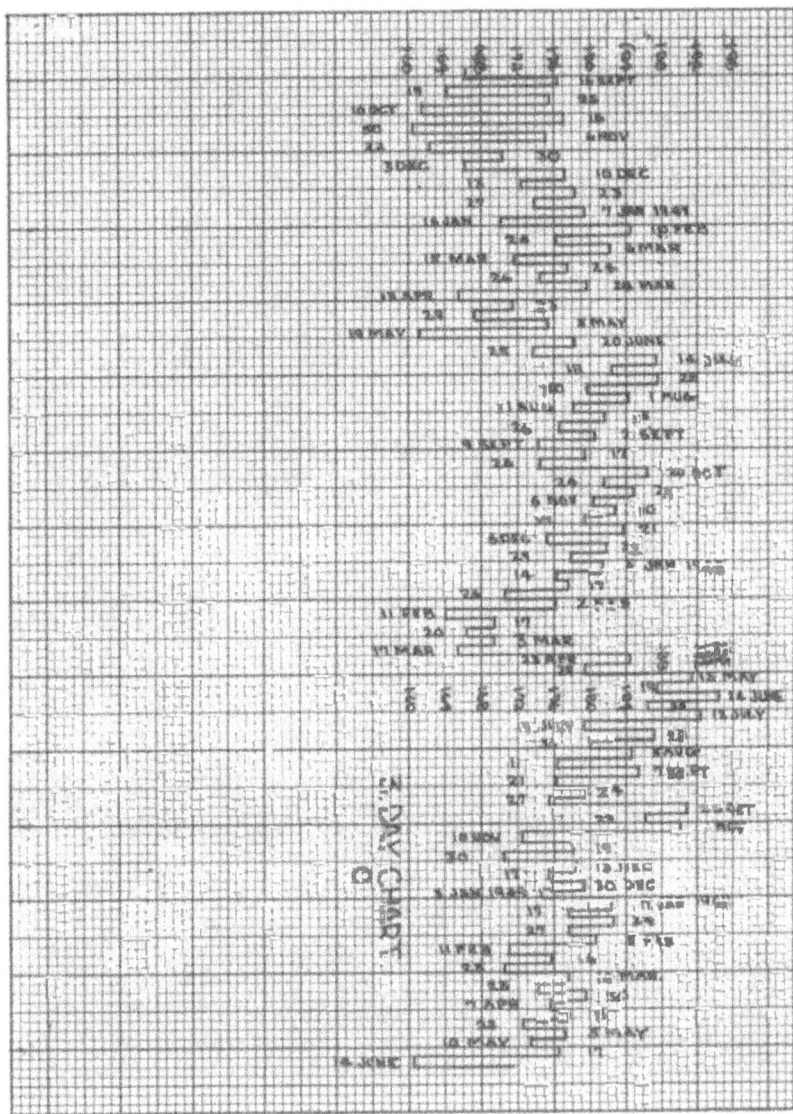

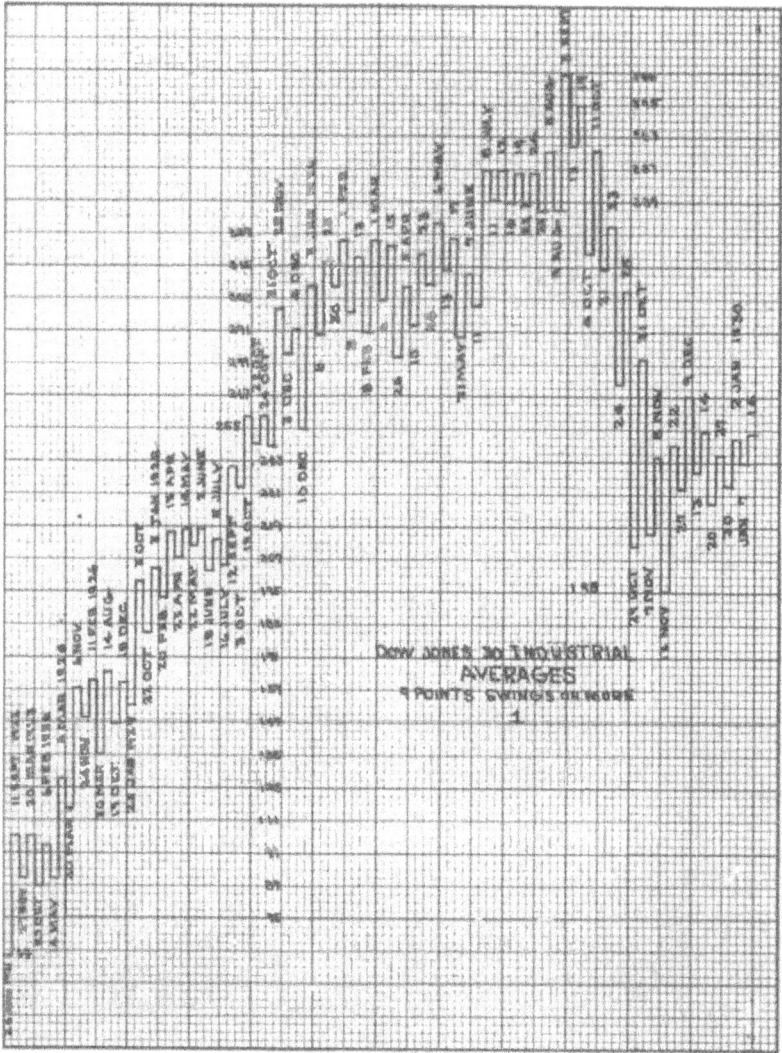

DOW JONES 30 INDUSTRIAL
AVERAGES
9 POINTS SWINGS OR MORE
1

9 POINTS SWINGS

POINTS SWINGS

9 POINTS SWINGS
4

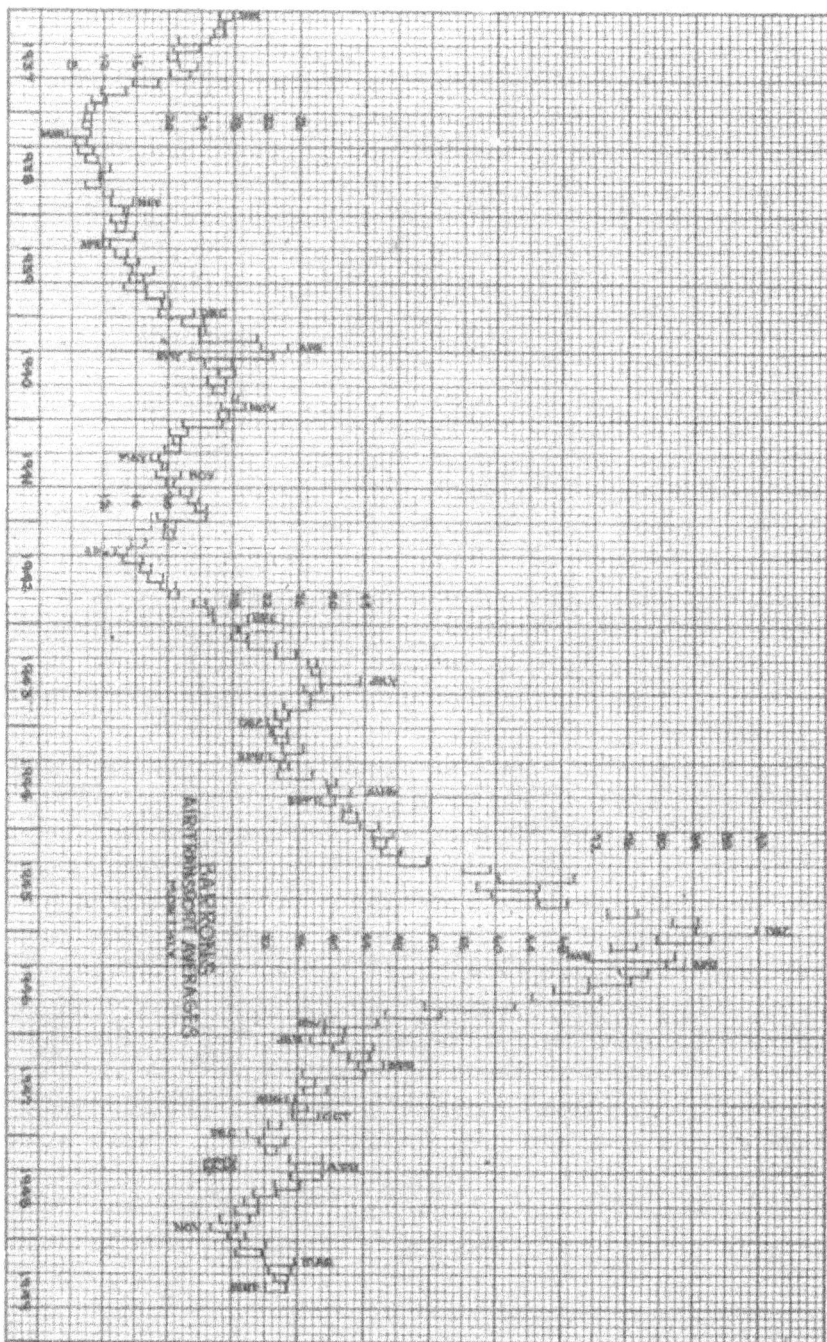

RAILROADS
A HISTORICAL AVERAGES
12 HR. LINE

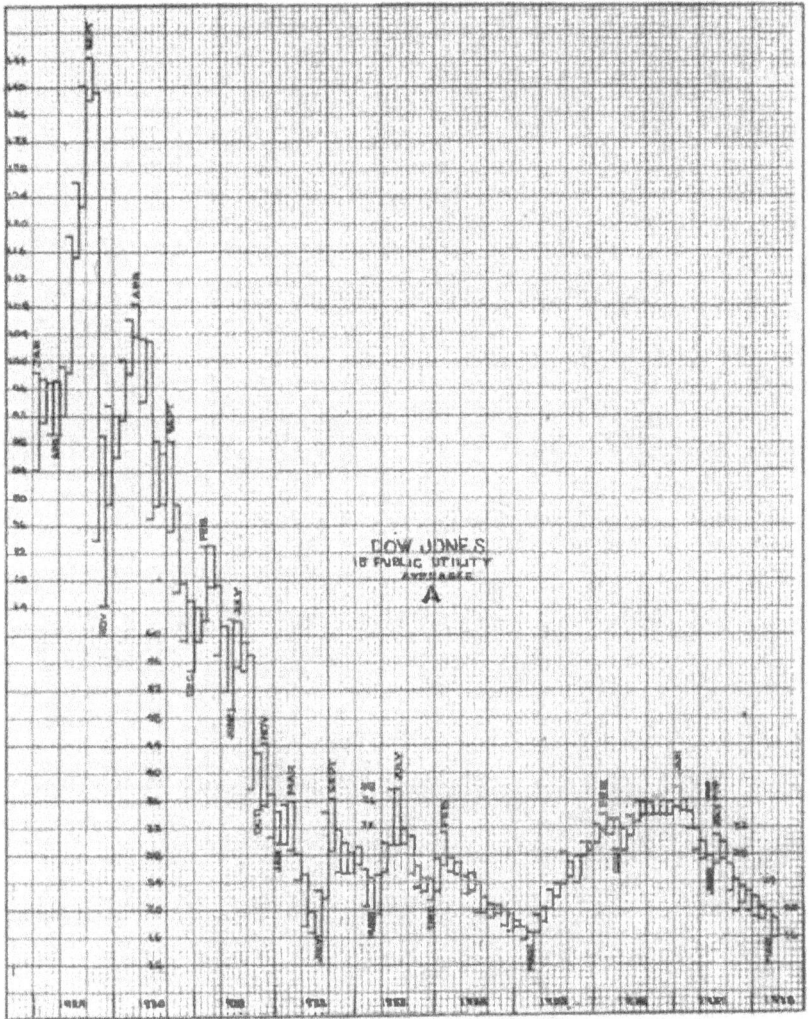

DOW JONES
15 PUBLIC UTILITY
AVERAGE
A

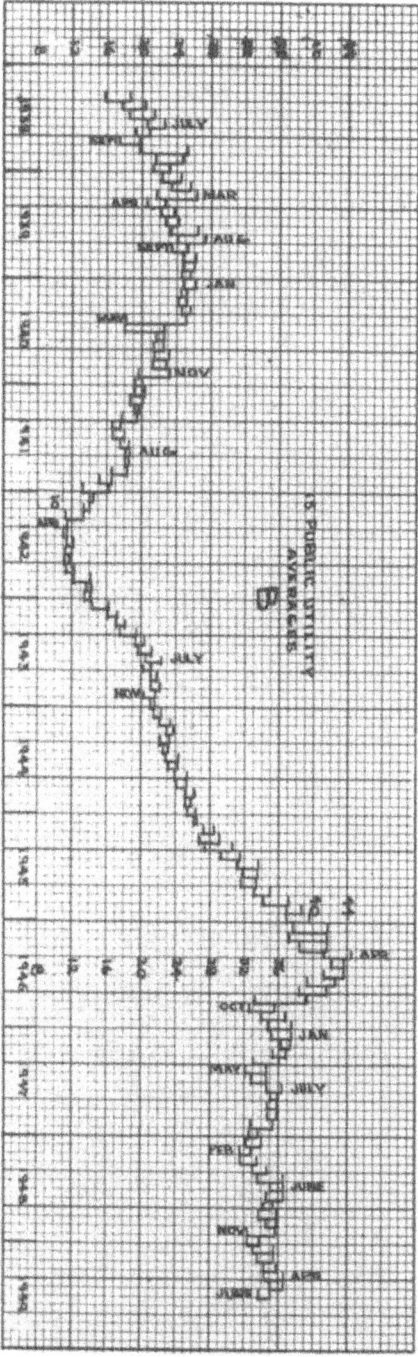

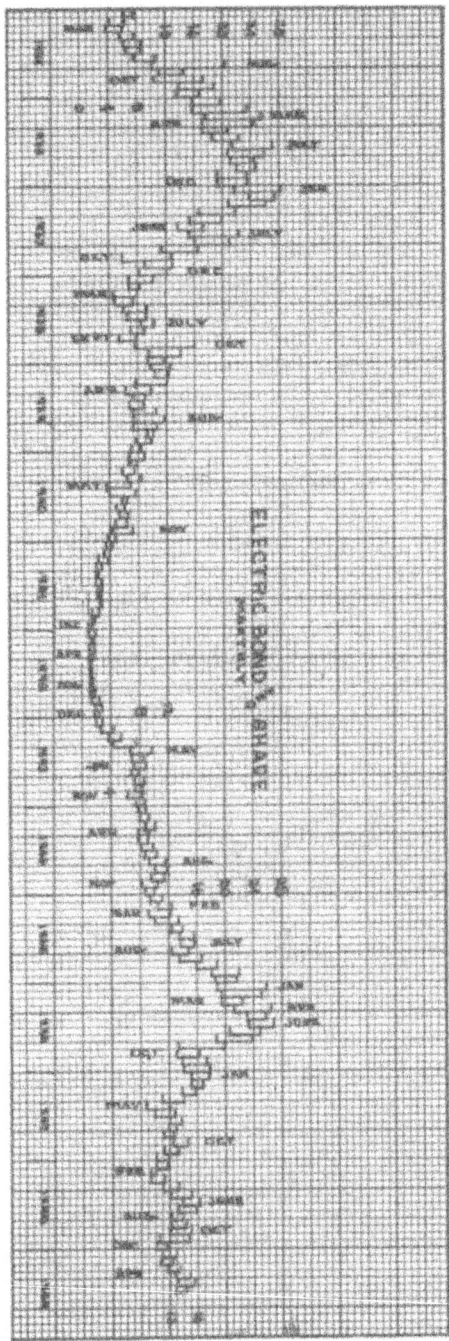

ELECTRIC BOND & SHARE
MONTHLY

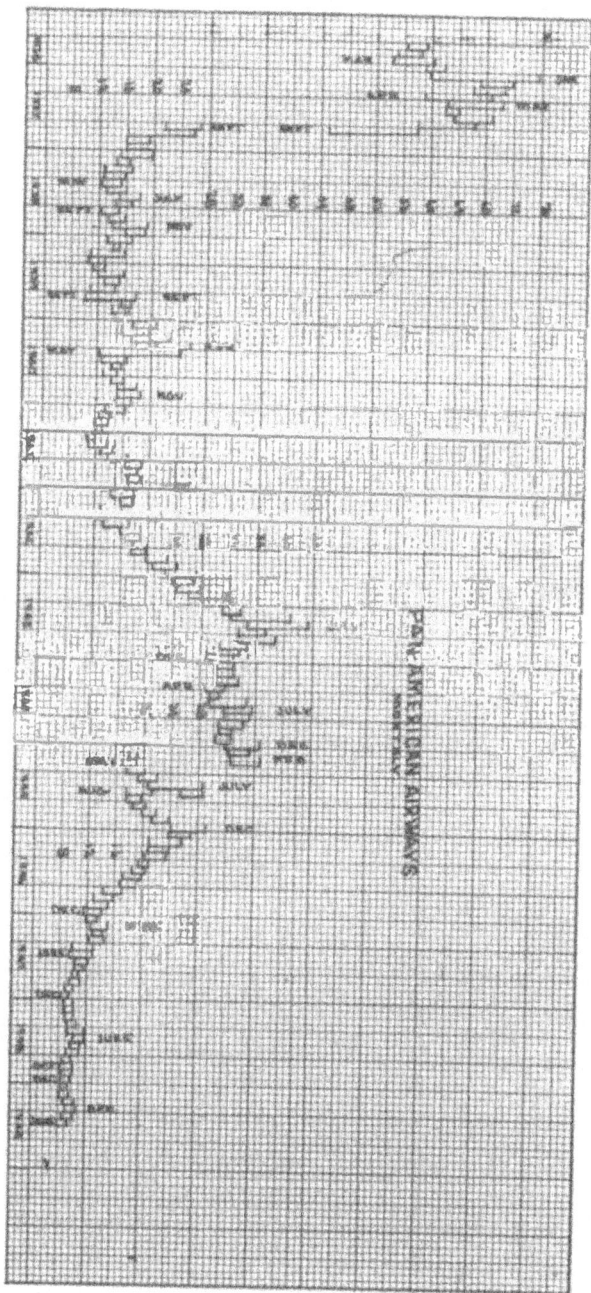

PAN AMERICAN AIRWAYS
SYSTEM

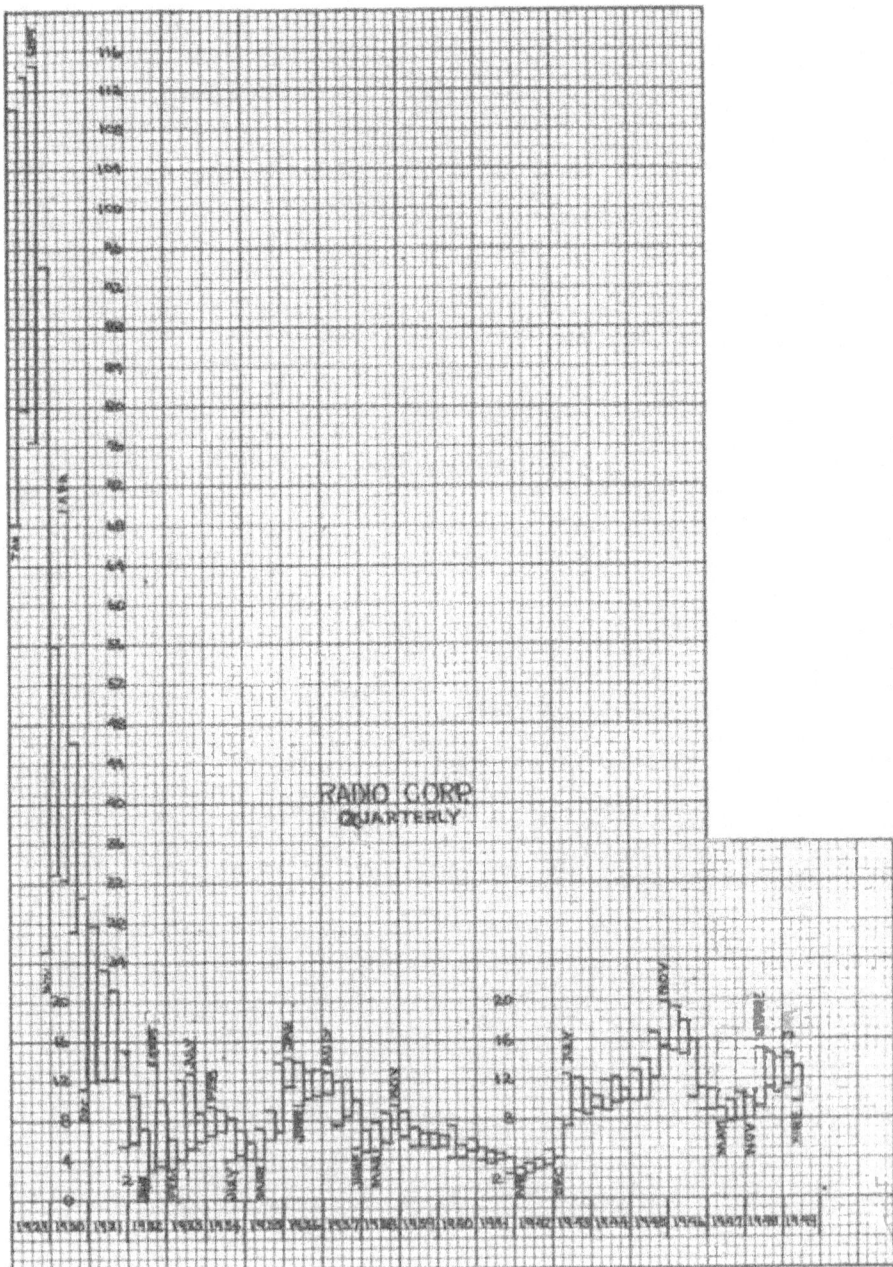

RADIO CORP
QUARTERLY

ANSWERS TO INQUIRIES

Hundreds of people write in from time to time asking for different kinds of information.   In order to avoid having to answer a lot of unnecessary correspondence, we are answering frequent inquiries below.

MAGAZINES

Many people write and ask what magazines we consider best for an investor or a trader to read.

We consider the *Magazine of Wall Street* one of the best magazines for information pertaining to the stock market. *B. C. Forbes Magazine* is also good. It contains many valuable articles on financial affairs. The *Annalist*, published weekly by the *New York Times*, specializes on financial affairs and contains information valuable to traders and investors.

NEWSPAPERS

Investors and traders often want to know what newspaper we consider best for them to read.

The Wall Street Journal—This is the best financial newspaper published. It specializes in presenting all facts and information pertaining to corporations throughout the country, as well as major foreign corporations.   Pertinent national news, especially agricultural and political, is equally stressed.   This was one of the first papers to publish a set of averages or railroad and industrial stocks.   These averages go back to 1896.   Since 1914, it has published an average of bond prices and, since 1928, a public utility stock average.   All of these averages are published daily and are very valuable to investors and traders who want to keep up charts on these various groups.   Another feature of the *Wall Street Journal* is that it publishes each day a list of stocks which make a new high for the year and a list that makes a new low for the year. The *Wall Street Journal* does not publish any tips, rumors or misleading information.   It publishes only reliable facts which are helpful to investors and traders.   From time to time the *Wall Street Journal* publishes various charts on stocks, which are very helpful to traders and would cost them a lot of money if they had to secure the records and make up the charts themselves.

The New York Herald Tribune—This paper carries averages on various groups of stocks, as well as other information which is helpful to traders.

The New York Times—This also has a special set of averages and is a good paper for investors and traders to read.

What investors and traders want are the facts about the different companies and reports, and not tips or rumors.   The newspapers, all of which are published in New York City, strive to give facts and reliable information.

STOCKS AND COMMODITIES

Baron's Magazine is one of the very good financial magazines published covering financial affairs and giving facts valuable to every investor and trader. The subscription rate is very low, compared to its value.   This magazine is published weekly and is well worth subscribing to.

Chicago Journal of Commerce—This paper covers the commodity field better than most any other newspaper. Continuous quotations are given daily on all grains traded in on the Chicago Board of Trade. Continuous quotations on eggs on the Chicago Mercantile Exchange are also reported. Stock prices are covered daily and weekly and all facts pertaining to stocks and commodities are covered and commented on by an able staff of writers.

Commodity Year Book, published by Commodity Research Bureau, Inc., 76 Beaver Street, New York City. This book covers general statistical information on almost every commodity, and is one of the best of its kind for reliable, accurate statistical information.

Odd Lot Trades In Stocks and Job Lots In Grain

Traders often inquire whether they can buy and sell odd lots of stocks. Most of the brokers who are members of the New York Stock Exchange accept orders for odd lots. Most of them will buy stocks outright or for cash in any amount from one share on up. Job lots or 1,000 bushels of grain are traded in on the Chicago Board of Trade. Some of the brokers handle job lots and some do not. You can inquire from any broker who is a member of the Chicago Board of Trade and find out about trading in job lots or less than 5,000 bushels, which is a round lot or a contract. The Chicago Board of Trade and New Orleans Cotton Exchange trade in 50 bales of cotton. No other reliable exchange will trade in less than 50 bale lots of cotton. Those that are trading in or soliciting business for odd lots of cotton in 10 bales or more are, as a rule, bucket shops. Traders should be careful about placing their accounts with firms who are not members of the leading stock exchanges or commodity exchanges.

Brokers

People write and ask if we consider such and such a firm of brokers reliable. We consider all members of the New York Stock Exchange, the New York Cotton Exchange and the Chicago Board of Trade reliable, and advise traders to always keep their accounts with members of these responsible exchanges. If in doubt about your broker, get a report through Bradstreet, R. G. Dunn, or Bishop Service. For Brokers not members of one of the leading Exchanges, you should get a private report through your banker or some commercial agency before placing your account with them. You might be trading with a bucket shop and not know it.

NOTES

NOTES

www.ingramcontent.com/pod-product-compliance
Lightning Source LLC
Chambersburg PA
CBHW040826300326
41914CB00058B/1191